JUSTICE DENIED

JUSTICE DENIED

POLITICS
PERJURY
AND
PREJUDICE
IN THE LOTTERY

TINA LEWIS

ELDERBERRY PRESS

ELDERBERRY PRESS
1393 Old Homestead Road, Second Floor
Oakland, Oregon 97462—9506
editor@elderberrypress.com
TEL/FAX:541.459.6043

Publisher's Catalog-in-Publication Data
Justice Denied/Tina Lewis
ISBN: 1-930859-12-0
1. Gambling.
2. Whistle blowers.
3. Government
4. Corruption
5. Lottery
I. Title

This book was written, printed, and bound in the United States of America

"An honest man's the noblest work of God."

Robert Burns

To Blaine, who will always be my love and my hero…

This book is truly a labor of love.

TIME LINE

1973	Blaine becomes assistant director of Connecticut Lottery, one of seven Units of the Division of Special Revenue
1980	Blaine becomes unit chief of Connecticut Lottery
1981-86	A. W. (Fred) Oppenheimer is Executive Director of the Division of Special Revenue
1986	Orlando Ragazzi and Roland Lange appointed to Gaming Policy Board, a five member board which oversees all seven units of the Division ofSpecial Revenue
1987	William Hickey and Bruce Cowen appointed to Gaming Policy Board
1987-1989	Orlando Ragazzi is Executive Director of the Division of Special Revenue
January 1988	General Instrument awarded Lottery on-line contract
May 8, 1988	General Instrument goes on-line
May 18, 1988	Gag order issued
June 8, 1988	The Legislature's Program Review and Investigations Committee meets, and motion to investigate gag order and awarding of contract to General Instrument is defeated on party lines
May 9, 1988	State Police Investigation begins
Nov. 9, 1988	State Police Investigation ends
Jan. 4, 1989	Gag order partially rescinded
Jan. 10, 1989	State Police report released
April 26, 1989	William Hickey becomes Executive Director of the Division of Special Revenue, leaving only two members on the Gaming Policy Board

May 15, 1989 Hickey orders Blaine to misrepresent himself to the Gaming Policy Board by recommending a change in lotto making it far more difficult to win

May 16, 1989 Hickey repeats order for Blaine to misrepresent himself before the Gaming Policy Board and orders Blaine to remain silent about the order

May 17, 1989 Hickey repeats orders to misrepresent himself and to remain silent. Blaine gives detailed reasons why Hickey should withdraw order to misrepresent himself

May 18, 1989 Blaine put on leave

May 22, 1989 Hickey gives Blaine notice of Loudermill Hearing for May 24, 1989. Blaine's request for more time to prepare and obtain counsel rejected

May 23, 1989 Request for more time by Blaine's counsel also rejected

May 24, 1989 Loudermill Hearing

May 25, 1989 Blaine's counsel notified of Meeting of Gaming Policy Board as it was already starting

May 26, 1989 Blaine is terminated at the extension of the Gaming Policy Board meeting

Nov. 1989 Superior Court Judge Samuel Freed rules that Blaine has a "contested case" under the Connecticut Statutes of the Uniform Administrative Procedure Act

Nov. 1991 Superior Court Judge Raymond Norko was to decide whether Blaine was entitled to damages and reinstatement, but instead he revisits Judge Freed's decision on jurisdictional grounds and reverses it.

May 7, 1992 Blaine has a heart attack and two weeks later a cerebral hemorrhage

Oct. 1992 Appeal to the Connecticut Supreme Court

Feb. 1993 Decision by the Connecticut Supreme Court upholding Judge Norko

Feb. 1993	Blaine develops simple partial seizure disorder two days later
June 1995	Blaine has a stroke robbing him of his speech
Nov. 1995	Blaine has open heart, by-pass surgery
May 1996	Blaine hospitalized with heart failure
Dec.12, 1996	Blaine vindicated in Trial in Federal District Court
Jan. 15, 1999	Reversal by 2nd Circuit Court of Appeals
Oct. 1999	Blaine's petition to the U.S. Supreme Court denied

CONTENTS

BACKGROUND

I am writing this book for Blaine. He so wanted a book written about the injustice he endured due to political influence, the Courts of the State of Connecticut, and the 2nd Circuit Court of Appeals. The impact of the injustice not only shattered our lives, but it affects all state managers and therefore the lives of all citizens. Blaine would often give an example that if a state manager thought that a bridge was structurally unsound and his boss told him to report it being safe, lying would be the only way to keep his job.

In the months before I lost Blaine he often spoke of his desire for such a book. He felt badly that I as his caregiver had little time for the endeavor, and he due to his illness had little energy. He was only able to write a few pages in a notebook and that in his own words is how the story of his struggle begins. I started writing while he was still alive and he was grateful and pleased with the results. He was so concerned about my health and felt so guilty about my efforts as his caregiver that he wanted me to obtain a ghostwriter and a literary agent to help me. After I lost Blaine, I found that his spirit lived on in me and I found that writing this book gave me the great satisfaction of doing something for him. It had the additional benefit of being wonderful therapy for me. It gave me something to live for at a time when my world had collapsed.

As I write this several months have passed since Blaine's funeral, and I am overwhelmed and devastated. I had never fully realized how much I lived for the two of us as a team and how little meaning life would have without him. My life was centered on Blaine. I was his caregiver since May 1992, and since then we never were apart. When we did our grocery shopping he would push the cart for me. Before he was able to do that he would wait in the car with a walkie-talkie so that he could call

13

me if needed. He never complained and always worked hard to recover from his many health set-backs. He never lost his quick wit, his interest in people and politics or his wonderful sense of humor.

Blaine died in the Neurosurgical Intensive care unit of the Hartford Hospital after seven weeks and one day. He was unconscious. I only hope he did not suffer and that he may have sensed my presence and that it may have been comforting. I would comb his hair and shave him with his electric shaver. I would talk to him on the chance that he could hear me and I played CD's of his favorite music. I would tell him how handsome he was and how very much I loved him. For seven weeks and one day I held his hand and hoped that he would wake up, and then he could fight off all his health problems. It was not to be.

Blaine's Struggle in His Own Words

"Where should the book start? Answer 1980. In 1980 I had been Assistant Director of the Connecticut State Lottery for 7 years, when the politicians decided to reorganize the state's legalized gambling. It then consisted of the State lottery, Off-track betting, and a third unit with Dog racing & Jai Alai, with lottery providing approximately 90% of the net revenue to the State.

Consultants were hired to determine how the state legalized gambling should be organized. Not surprisingly they recommended many changes. The nine Commissioners of Special Revenue, who were appointed by the Governor and approved by the Legislature, were replaced by 5 members of a Gaming Policy Board to be appointed and approved in the same manner. Only one experienced with consultants and who knows how bureaucrats enjoy working could understand the logic of the next change. The three operating units were replaced by 7 units. The additional units consisted of Security, Administration, Planing & Research, and Licensing & Integrity Assurance.

There were other changes. The position of Executive Secretary of the Division of Special Revenue (DOSR) changed to "Executive Director" of the DOSR. The titles of the Executive Directors of the three operating units were changed to "Unit Heads" and those in charge of the newly created units were made "Unit Heads".

The Governor appointed John Devine, a retired FBI man as the new Executive Director of the DOSR. He was a fine gentleman who I am sure was a good FBI man, but he had exactly zero lottery experience. My boss, John Winchester, who had been Executive Director of the Lottery resigned.

One of the first decisions John Devine was required to make was to find a Unit Head for the Lottery which made most of the net revenue. I don't know if John Devine made this decision unaided, but I believe he probably made the decision himself because the Democrats were in power in the state, and I was a Republican. The only thing I know for sure was that I never asked for the position and that it was offered to me by John Devine.

I have been asked why I did not lobby for the position. My only answer is that perhaps I felt more secure being protected from the disaster produced from politicians who would be calling the shots in running a large business. When offered the position I could not resist. I had no way of knowing that the disaster would ultimately be much more serious to me and to all state managers throughout the country.

The Governor appointed the five members of the newly created Gaming Policy Board (GPB). The GPB permitted me to operate the Lottery in the manner I desired and John Devine paid little attention to the Lottery, and it continued to prosper. For some reason, which I never understood, John Devine left rather quickly. To replace John Devine, Governor Grasso appointed another FBI man, Harold Bassett." (End of Blaine's writing)

Blaine's Story Continued by the Author

Bassett did not remain long as Executive Director either.

Even though Blaine felt Bassett's relationship with everyone at the Division was a bit strained, once he announced his leaving he had an uncharacteristically warm and friendly visit with Blaine in Blaine's office. Blaine was grateful for the warm farewell, but not sorry to see him depart.

The next Executive Director to be appointed was A. W. (Fred) Oppenheimer. He remained in that post from 1981 through 1986. Blaine had a great deal of respect for Oppenheimer and felt he was financially knowledgeable and competent. He, in turn, respected Blaine and did not try to micromanage the Lottery. The only time that Blaine complained was when he was anxious to start a lotto game and had to put it on hold. Oppenheimer wanted to have a weekly television show and felt that was a better way to increase revenues. Up to that point the drawings were done "on the road", weekly events in different places in the state. There was no animosity. In fact there was "The Bet". Blaine predicted that weekly sales would be $275,000 or less. William T. Drakeley, who was Deputy Executive Director, predicted that weekly sales would be $350,000 or more. They each put up one dollar, 5 witnesses were listed and with Oppenheimer's signature, it was dated May 6, 1981.[1] "The Bet" was framed and hung in Oppenheimer's office.

The weekly televised show was a big effort since it had to be designed so that it would be interesting but not exceed the half-hour time slot. A lot of talented people from the television industry helped make the show a success. But as good as it was, Blaine's sales predictions proved correct. When Oppenheimer became disillusioned with the sales figures, the television show was withdrawn and Blaine was allowed to start what was to be a very successful Lotto game. Blaine was sorry that so much time had been lost but thrilled to design and implement a Lotto game which was introduced in 1983.

Oppenheimer was replaced by Orlando Ragazzi as Executive Director and Ragazzi was in that position when the important on-line contract went out to bid in 1987. Ragazzi had been a member of the Gaming Policy Board for about one year and before that had held a high rank in the State Police. He had little lottery experience.

Blaine always felt that the pressure he endured from Ragazzi to favor General Instrument with the new lotto, daily numbers and play 4 on-line contract was a politically orchestrated move. Based on General Instrument's record of performance in other states, Blaine felt the state was putting itself at great risk by awarding them the contract. Time proved him right. In addition, American Totalisator, a subsidiary of General Instrument, had the state's Off-track betting contract for 16 years without competitive bid. Blaine felt that it was an uncomfortable relationship and did not want the lottery to suffer as a result.

The five members of the Gaming Policy Board usually met once a month and were responsible for overseeing all state gaming, including the lottery. No new actions such as a change in games or lottery vendors, and hiring or firing a unit chief, such as Blaine, could take place without their vote of approval. Their compensation for each meeting was $50. They did not have the knowledge or experience to micromanage any of the various Units in the Division, but each of several disciplines were to be represented thereby creating an effective oversight on state gaming.

Orlando Ragazzi and Roland Lange became members of the Board in 1986. William Hickey became a member of the Board in 1987 when Ragazzi became Executive Director of the Division. Thomas Barrett had resigned and was replaced by Bruce Cowen. Hickey, Cowen and Lange, as members of the Board, all voted to award the on-line contract to GI.

In early 1989, when Stanley J. Pribyson died, there were only three remaining members on the Board, Hickey, Cowen and Lange. Ragazzi resigned as Executive Director in early 1989 due to health reasons, and he was replaced with Hickey. This left two members on the Board. Despite the fact that a quorum of 4 was required for the Board to take any action, the remaining two members, Cowen and Lange anxiously voted to fire Blaine when Hickey recommended Blaine's dismissal based on his refusal to lie by recommending the change in lotto from 6 in 40 to 6 in 44. Hickey's order came two weeks after Governor William O'Neill had appointed him Executive Director. He requested the dismissal one month after his own appointment.

There was an opinion written by Assistant Attorney General Richard Sheridan and signed by acting Attorney General Clarine Nardi Riddle dated May 1, 1989. Sheridan was assigned to the Division of Special Revenue and volunteered that he had "authored" the opinion. The opinion was to reduce the quorum needed to take action from 4 members to 3; and then in a footnote the number was conveniently reduced to 2. Cowen and Lange admitted at the very Board meeting in which Blaine was fired that they had not seen or read the opinion. They had only been told about it. They all knew that Blaine had too much integrity to lie and they used that knowledge to get rid of him. Where was their integrity? Where was their responsibility to the state? Why were they so motivated?

A WIFE'S VIEW

Blaine was born on the 4th of July 1920, and had always been so proud to be an American. He believed in the American dream, he believed in the Constitution and he believed in our system of justice. His honesty, intelligence and integrity were assets in his everyday life that along with a tremendous capacity for hard work brought him success in all he touched. He had had a successful career in electrical engineering both as a consultant and then as part owner of a manufacturing firm.

His strong principles and ideals along with his quick thinking and exceptional ability to express himself made him a natural for public service. He proudly served his town of Glastonbury on the Sewer Commission, on the Board of Tax Review, and then on the Town Council. He always stuck to his principles with a great sense of civic pride.

In 1973 after several years of public service, he decided to get back into the job market. An opening as assistant to the chief of the Connecticut lottery in the state's Division of Special Revenue seemed an interesting challenge. Lotteries were new, only one year in Connecticut, and there were few people with lottery experience. With his mathematics background, his business knowledge, and his capacity to learn and manage, he proved to be a great asset to the Division and to the state.

After seven years as assistant, Blaine became chief of the lottery in 1980. He was conscientious and took great pride in the success of the lottery. He now had expertise in lotteries, he was devoted to his job, he was honest and he was always a gentleman. His enthusiasm was contagious and he happily gave a lot of his own time promoting the lottery and creating good will. He was a sought after speaker accepting invitations from many organizations such as the Elks, Rotary, Civitan, and Lions Clubs. He was also a speaker at a men's Catholic Church meeting as well as an Italian-American club meeting. These appearances were always evenings or weekends, but he gladly drove himself there, covering the whole state, doing it on his own time.

Blaine was a guest on many radio talk shows from New London to New Haven to Fairfield county and Hartford. The shows were so successful that he was usually invited back. He felt it was important to answer people's questions about the games, the odds of winning, new games on the horizon, or anything else of concern about the lottery.

His relationship with the press was good. He was open and honest and never failed to give as much time as was necessary to answer questions, even when it involved being called at home. He understood that it was easy to forget to ask some questions in an interview and he was anxious that reports of a new game or drawing be correct. In 1989 he was awarded the Helen M. Loy Freedom of Information Award by the Connecticut Society of Professional Journalists

Being involved with drawings and security was part of his job, but he felt the perception of fairness was also important. Blaine wanted to show all the numbered balls before they went into a mixing chamber and then drawn into tubes. He designed and built a prototype machine in his own home workshop, evenings on his own time. It took one to two months but he was then able to get the machines he wanted for the drawings.

His hard work and managerial skills certainly contributed to sales and state revenues increasing every year, with sales quadrupling from 1980 to 1988 when he was chief of the lottery.

Blaine reported to the Executive Director and the Gaming Policy Board. They were responsible for policy decisions. Even though there had been many different Executive Directors and many changes on the Gaming Policy Board, Blaine worked well with his superiors and followed orders with which he did not always agree.

When Blaine recommended the state have a lotto game to replace the weekly game that had been on the road, his superiors at that time disagreed. They preferred having a weekly lottery game show on television. Blaine was correct in his assessment of how successful lotto would be but he respected and got on well with his superiors and he followed orders. When it became apparent that the weekly television show was not meeting their sales expectations, the show was dropped and replaced with lotto. Lotto, which proved to be very successful had been delayed one year and began in 1983.

When Blaine wanted to join a multi-state lotto game, Lotto America that began in 1988, his superiors said no. Lotto America evolved into Powerball and Connecticut eventually did join seven years later in 1995 when Blaine was no longer there.

In 1987, the contract for an on-line vendor went out to bid. The performance of their current vendor, G Tech was excellent. General Instrument submitted a bid that was $11 million less for a 5-year contract. Blaine calculated that a drop of 1.2% in sales would wipe out the theoretical savings. Blaine had been called as a witness to testify in a New Jersey hearing about his experience with G Tech. While there he heard about many problems that New Jersey had experienced with General Instrument. Even though General Instrument was the low bidder in New Jersey, their contract was not renewed. Blaine became concerned about General Instrument and looked into its experience and performance in other states.

Ohio had also failed to renew General Instrument's contract despite their low bid. The only state where General Instrument had a lottery contract was Missouri. There, GI was not only losing money, but Missouri was suing GI.

The OTB contract had gone to GI for 16 years with no bids. Blaine felt the state had an uncomfortable relationship with GI and did not want the lottery damaged as a result. Blaine took pride in the lottery being well run and felt frustrated and upset about the pending disaster with GI. He felt anyone with an open mind would understand the error about to be made. Blaine was thrilled when the Executive Director set up a meeting with the Chairman of the Board in order that Blaine could explain his concerns. After all, state law requires the contract go to the lowest, *qualified* bidder.

Blaine had written a memo to the assistant in the state purchasing department detailing all his concerns.[1] Blaine gave the Chairman 5 copies of his memo at their meeting and was reassured by the Chairman that all 5 members of the Board would get a copy and address his concerns. Blaine was thrilled with the Chairman's reaction and felt that now reason would prevail. When he called me from work the next day he was stunned. GI had received the Board's vote without any discussion of his memo and objections or any mention of the objections from others.[2] When he returned to his office, the Executive Director phoned him to tell him that he was not to discuss the contract with anyone. Blaine felt betrayed. The Chairman had not lived up to Blaine's expectations. He had not done as he had promised. Blaine was left to wonder why.

Once the contract was awarded in early 1988, Blaine worked to make the best of it. There was frequent talk at home about GI's inability to get things right with the testing done by the Division's accounting department. When they corrected a glitch, it would frequently cause a glitch in another previously passed test. Their inability to pass the testing was very frustrating to Blaine and the accounting department.[3] Blaine frequently talked about his frustration with the testing and how GI complained that the Division was being unreasonable. Blaine felt GI was trying to get away with incompetence.

As the time approached for GI to go on-line, May 8, 1988, Blaine was worried about an impending disaster.[4] So were others in the accounting department who were responsible for the testing.[5] He wanted to postpone GI going on-line until they were ready. It was like a bad dream, but it was a decision to be made by his superiors, the Executive Director and the Gaming Policy Board. They were the policy-makers, not Blaine.

I felt so badly for him when GI was allowed to go on-line and the system quickly crashed. He tried in his first press interviews to minimize the problems and even made excuses for GI. He hoped that GI would miraculously correct all the multiplying problems. Blaine soon gave up all hope for a quick system correction and decided to answer his press questions honestly. He felt it was his duty to the public to tell the truth.

GI could be replaced by G Tech who had been asked by

the state to stand by for just such an occurrence. Blaine could not understand why at least the temporary option was not taken in light of the devastation to lotto and the other on-line games.[6] His superiors, instead of doing what was right for the citizens of the state, decided to silence him. He was very upset by the gag order.[8] There was a transparent attempt to disguise the purpose of the order by making it apply to all unit heads. An official spokesman for the Division was appointed and Blaine was prohibited from speaking publicly. He was thus deprived of his right of free speech violating both the First Amendment of the U.S.Constitution and Article First of the Connecticut Constitution.

During this period of time, William V. Hickey, who later became Executive Director, Bruce D. Cowen and Roland H. Lange were all on the Gaming Policy Board. They all had voted to award the on-line contract to GI. Not one of the three had objected to GI going on-line despite all the warnings. Not one of the three had objected to the gag order.

Hickey was sworn in as chairman of the Gaming Policy Board on August 24, 1988, with Governor O'Neill by his side. According to published reports, he said he supported the order barring the head of lottery games from talking to the media, and that he saw nothing wrong with the directive.

The General Assembly's Program Review and Investigations Committee met on June 8, 1988, one month after the initial on-line lottery problems. Before the meeting started two interesting people entered the chamber and made the rounds of committee members. One was Paddi Leshane of Sullivan & Leshane, GI's lobbyists in Connecticut. The other, David McQuade, was one of Governor O'Neill's top aids.

Republican State Senator Fred Lovegrove of Fairfield expressed concern about the gag order and wondered what Blaine might have to say. It was disappointing to hear liberal Democrat State Senator Richard Blumenthal and Democrat State Representative Richard Mulready of West Hartford rise to attack Blaine. Richard Blumenthal said the gag order "did not merit their time" and that Blaine was "free to resign as a matter of conscience…if he feels the restrictions are unwarranted." Mulready spoke in the same vane and said Blaine could leave if he didn't like it. He said the future would prove who was right. It sure did, Mr.Mulready, and that was Blaine. Where was Blumenthal's concern for Blaine's 1st amendment right of free speech or does that not matter when that free speech conflicts with your political party's interest? What about the interests of the citizens of your state? Even the Connecticut Civil Liberties Union expressed concern. Seven months later [in January 1989] the CCLU threatened to sue the state over the gag order, and that resulted in the gag order being modified to allow Blaine to speak to the press as long as he made it clear that he was not speaking for the lottery.[9] Blaine referred to that as his "Surgeon General's warning". At that time Blaine was president of NASPL (North American Association of State and Provincial Lotteries). He could speak for every Canadian lottery and every state lottery except his own.

When Lovegrove, at that committee meeting, made a motion to publicly question gaming officials about the lottery problems, the vote was defeated on party lines, six Democrats including Blumenthal and Mulready to four Republicans. That was the same Richard Blumenthal who years later, as Attorney General for the state of Connecticut, in this writer's opinion, submitted lies and fabrications in an appeal to the 2nd Circuit Court of Appeals.[14] It was those very lies and fabrications that were the basis for the reversal in Blaine's 1996 victory in his trial in Federal District Court.[15] It is difficult, if not impossible, to believe that the appeal was filed without his knowledge and authority. The reversal defied truth, testimony under oath, court exhibits and the law. Justice and political agendas proved incompatible.

Blaine did his best to track down errors and point out specific problems in order to improve the system. Problems existed with the modem, printer, mark reader, power supply and paper transport. All 2200 new terminals had to be rebuilt, a few at a time. This was not completed until April 1989, almost one year later. Lotto sales for the final quarter of 1988 were down 37.9 % from the previous year. The resulting drop in Lotto sales had to be an embarrassment to General Instrument, Hickey, Cowen and Lange.

On September 15,1988 an undated, unsigned report entitled "Lotto Lottery Sales Trends" had been presented to the Legislature's Public Safety Committee. It was 7 pages long with another 7 pages in the appendix. The report analyzed the lotto sales trends through August 9, 1988. By the continual use of "declining growth rate" and "declining lottery sales growth", the report gave the impression that the recent decline in lottery sales (due to the May 8 change in the on-line system) was nothing new. In Blaine's memo of October 11, 1988[7] he wrote, "It is true that before the installation of the new on-line system we had a declining growth rate. (After enjoying a 35% annual growth rate, it is very difficult to avoid a declining growth rate.) However, since the installation of the new system, we have had declining sales *—there is a difference.*"

From lotto's initial start up in November 1983 sales had always increased for each fiscal year. It was only to be expected that the biggest percent increases would be in the initial years. Despite the catastrophic GI problems in 1988, gross lotto sales for fiscal year 1987-88 were $259.4 million compared to $246.5 million in fiscal 1986-87. Fiscal years end the week of June 30 so that fiscal 87-88 included two months of hard hit sales. Of all state lotteries,Connecticut still ranked #1 for per capita lotto sales for fiscal year 1987-88.

Never before had a vendor designed any of the lottery games. They had always been designed by the lottery unit. Blaine found it difficult to believe that the very company that had caused so many problems in the recent past was now trying to blame the 6 of 40 Lotto game for those problems. He found it troubling to see how much influence GI had with the Division of Special Revenue.

Blaine was upset when GI proposed to change the lotto game in the fall of 1988. He felt they were trying to cover up their responsibility for the recent decline in sales. It was easier for them to blame Blaine's design of the lotto game. GI wanted to make the lotto twice as hard to win by going from 6 of 40 numbers to 6 of 44. That would drastically reduce the odds of winning from 1 in 3.8 million to 1 in 7.2 million. Even as sales recovered, GI's public relations people, Sullivan and LeShane went to newspaper editorial boards and to people in state government to promote the change. Blaine questioned the propriety of that and felt that GI was overstepping their state contract.

By February 1989, as the rebuilding of terminals was nearing completion, sales were breaking records established before GI had become the on-line vendor. The only change that had been necessary to restore sales was to fix the on-line system. Blaine felt the proposed change would hurt sales and revenues to the state. Our evenings were spent worrying about the proposed change and the continuing problems with the GI system. The Board had voted to give the contract to GI, and the Executive Director had let GI go on line when they were not ready. Blaine now hoped that, despite GI's influence, they would not want to be responsible for yet another disaster.

NASPL, The North American Association of State and Provincial Lotteries, was having a spring conference in Boston, Massachusetts April 1 – 4 in 1989. Lottery people from all US lotteries as well as all Canadian lotteries were in attendance as well as representatives of the lotteries of Ireland, Puerto Rico and the Virgin Islands. Since many lotteries sent their marketing and sales, advertising, and financial people as well as their directors, there were approximately 134 people representing the various lotteries. These conferences were (and still are) a forum for the exchange of ideas and information. There were many lectures ("presentations") and discussion groups for the benefit of the attendees. It was an effective way for lottery people to learn from the experiences of other lotteries. Blaine had always attended these conferences in the past as lottery chief. It was part of his job and beneficial to the state. There never had been any problem or hesitation in granting him permission to attend.

At this time, Blaine was the President of NASPL and with the duties and responsibilities that went with that office, his attendance was far more critical. April 1 and 2 were weekend days and would be on his own personal time. He would be on state time for 2 days only, April 3 and 4. He put in his request for this routine business trip but was astonished to discover that the approval had been denied. It was an insult to Blaine and to NASPL. There was no reimbursement for expenses or time allowed for the conference. Blaine used his own vacation days and paid for whatever expenses he incurred out of his own pocket. He was fortunate with regard to hotel expenses since NASPL provided him with a suite with a conference room for his necessary meetings as president. His political bosses in the state of Connecticut had sunk to a new low.

On April 26, 1989, Hickey, who was then a member of the Gaming Policy Board, was appointed by Governor William O'Neill to become Executive Director of the Division of Special Revenue. This left 2 members and 3 vacancies on the Gaming Policy Board. Hickey had been Executive Director for approximately 2 weeks when he ordered Blaine to present the lotto change to the 2 member Board,[10] With his deputy present on both May 15 and May 16, Hickey orally ordered Blaine to make the presentation in a positive, favorable manner, knowing that he could not honestly comply. Blaine felt it necessary to lay out all his reasons for his opposition to the game change and to the order itself.[11]

He recoiled at being told to present the game in a positive manner. Hickey was ordering him to lie by recommending the change. His honesty and reputation were being put in jeopardy. Blaine was so upset that I often called him at work to see how he was doing. He felt strongly that the change would do great damage, and he certainly was not going to lie and hide his concerns. We could only wonder why this was happening.

On May 15, there had been no action or advice from the Board. Blaine was unaware of the private, illegal meeting in Hickey's office where the three had agreed on the change. Asking Blaine to lie was unnecessary. It was to suppress his free speech and give an excuse for firing him when he predictably declined to lie.

Blaine was not warned that he would be suspended or terminated if he refused to lie. On May 18, 1989, the same week as the original order to lie, and with no notice, Blaine was put on leave. He phoned to tell me what had happened and that he would be home early. He was upset and did not want to talk to anyone. I began receiving calls from the press asking to speak to Blaine. When told he was not home from work, they diplomatically told me that they had heard rumors that there was a problem with his job. I told them I expected him home because we were going out that evening. We had tickets for the Bushnell that evening to see the musical, "Cats" (it was my Valentine's Day gift). Blaine had been ordered not to talk to the press about the order to change the game, and he had not. We decided going out was the best way to get his thoughts and emotions together and postpone questions from the press.

The next day, Friday, May 19, Blaine got a phone call from Hickey's secretary telling him to appear at Hickey's office on Monday, May 22. No reason was given. On Monday, I waited in the car when he went in, and when he came out of the meeting he was upset. Up to that point he felt he would not be fired, but the notice he was given for a pretermination hearing (Loudermill Hearing) for *two days* later, May 24, pursuant to the Division's Personnel Procedure No. 1 on the charge that he had refused to comply with an order noted that termination was being considered.[12]

Many state laws, Statutes and Division procedures had been violated and he felt he needed a lawyer. His request for more time to get a lawyer was denied. Blaine was used to putting up a good front, even with me, but there was a feeling of outrage at what they were doing to him and frustration that they were not being fair and setting him up. He no longer even tried to hide it. Blaine called an attorney friend, Bill Rogers and we went to his office. Despite the short notice, Bill agreed to represent him.

Blaine still had hopes for justice when he went to the pretermination hearing on May 24, at the Division of Special Revenue. I was proud of him. Despite his feelings he kept a smile on his face as he approached the building where members of the press were waiting on the stairway. He acted the same way when it was over, thirty to forty minutes later.

The hearing violated legal requirements and procedures under Personnel Procedure No.1:

a) The Hearing was to be conducted *before* a decision to discipline was made. Hickey later admitted under oath that he would have terminated Blaine without the hearing if he had had his way.

b) The Hearing was to be conducted by the responsible decision maker who must be open-minded. Hickey could not be open-minded since it was his order that had been disobeyed, and he admitted under oath that he would not have bothered with the Hearing. He had been advised to "stress" that he was open-minded in order to "cover" himself, in conducting the Hearing.

c) Blaine's request for additional time to prepare and obtain counsel was denied.

d) The Hearing was not open to the public as requested by Blaine, and therefore Hickey's decision was unlawful.

e) There were no oaths administered, and no witnesses or cross-examination allowed.

At the Hearing Blaine stated that he was, and always had been willing to obey all lawful orders, including the order to design the new Lotto game and to present it in an objective way with all relevant facts to the Board. At the Hearing, Blaine through counsel requested Hickey to notify him if the approval of Hickey's decision were added to the Board's agenda. It was not on the published agenda for the Board meeting the next day. It was added the next morning and Blaine's counsel was notified after the Board meeting had already started on May 25. Blaine had been put on leave and therefore was not present.

Blaine's assistant presented the change in Lotto to the 2 member Board in a favorable way with no risks mentioned, and as they had previously agreed, the 2 member Board approved the change. The Board then went into executive session to discuss Blaine's termination even though it had not been properly placed on the agenda. Blaine's counsel was notified at 2:55 p.m. that the executive session of the Board would be extended to the next day, May 26, ostensibly so that Blaine could be heard.

The notice to both the Loudermill Hearing and the Board meeting were both inadequate and unreasonable.

The extension of the Board hearing was devastating. Bruce Cowen and Roland Lange were the only 2 members of what was supposed to be a 5 member Board. Blaine and his counsel were not prepared for the rude, nasty, interrupting, patronizing behavior they received from Cowen and Lange. Blaine and his counsel were repeatedly interrupted and Blaine was prevented from giving his full prepared statement.[13] They never interrupted Hickey once during a long statement that often rambled on about unrelated matters. They did not ask to see any reports or documents concerning the pretermination hearing or anything that led up to or followed the hearing. In their haste to act they admitted that they had not even seen the acting Attorney General's opinion which stretching credibility said that 3 members instead of the quorum of 4 required by Statute could act as the Board. A footnote in the opinion extended the 3 members to 2 members. Why not 1? Why bother?

There were no oaths, Blaine was not allowed to have witnesses, or cross-examine witnesses. Without any public discussion and despite the fact that the Board had only 2 members when a quorum of 4 was required by Connecticut Statute, Cowen and Lange voted to terminate Blaine. It seemed obvious to Blaine they had made up their minds beforehand. Blaine as well as several members of the press called it a kangaroo court. Blaine had never suspected their personal animosity, and he was stunned.

After the termination Blaine was in a state of disbelief. As a result, he had trouble sleeping. He kept up a good front in public but he was quite distressed. He had given so much of himself to the lottery and he cared so much about its success. To be ordered to lie to bring about another lottery calamity was too much to cope with. He remained silent rather than lie and violate the public trust. He had to live with himself, and he had too much principal and character to behave otherwise. He not only had character but he was right. His prediction proved correct for a great loss in state revenues.

Going to the office to collect his personal belongings was

very difficult. We both kept smiling but had to work hard to hide our feelings. I was very proud of how he reacted to his humiliating treatment. The head of personnel, Alan Mazzola, stood by and checked each item that we put aside to take home. Several times he rushed over to see what I had put in a carton. We were taking personal items such as a toothbrush, an electric shaver, a comb, a plant that was a gift from his staff. We took several of our own pictures that we had framed ourselves including a few impressionist prints and an enlarged photo of me with my mother's cat by the ocean. His "Illegitimi Non Carborundum" sign that he always kept on his desk seemed incredibly appropriate. (Latin for Don't let the bastards grind you down)

At that time, Blaine was president of NASPL (North American Association of State and Provincial Lotteries), an organization with all the lottery states as well as lottery provinces of Canada as members. He therefore had a lot of NASPL paperwork and videos that he had to take. Mazzola insisted on looking at everything Blaine put into cartons. He treated us like thieves. He had been a long-time personal friend of Hickey's and that, in Blaine's opinion, had contributed to his behavior.

Some people from the Division came in to wish Blaine well. One of the lottery people brought us several cartons trying to be of help and of course it was appreciated. Another lottery employee kept pacing from his office into the hall disgusted with the turn of events and not afraid to express his feelings.

We carried the belongings out to the car in several trips feeling that everyone was staring at us, not only as we walked down the halls but also from their windows as we loaded Blaine's belongings into the car. There were members of the press in the parking lot taking pictures and asking questions. They wanted to enter the building in order to take pictures of Blaine's office being emptied. They were not allowed to do so. Almost twelve years have passed and the recollection of all these events remains so vivid.

Because Blaine and his attorney felt very strongly that the Board's action had been clearly illegal, he still had hopes that he could get his job back. That hope made his ordeal more bearable. Dozens of sympathetic letters and even poems from perfect strangers came in the mail. Another stranger sent a box made from a book, with an ocean scene with seashells, a porcelain bird and fish inside. The cover read "ILLEGITIMI NON CARBORUNDUM". I'm sure they had no idea how helpful their support was.

We saw many letters to the editor in the paper supporting Blaine, and these too helped his spirits. But the depression remained and the injustice was difficult to cope with.

Because of his age when he was fired, one month short of 69, moving to another state to use his lottery experience was not an appealing option. My mother who was in her 90's spent summers and many weekends with us and was very dependent on us. Blaine had wanted to work until his 72nd birthday, but at 69 it was not worth uprooting our lives and my mom's life too. Besides he felt that with any justice he should get his job back.

We had to explain the situation to my mother who was so upset when seeing the news coverage on television. She was so proud of Blaine and always told people how smart and honest her son-in-law was, and that he would be vindicated some day. She died in September 1993 and went to her grave without seeing that day.

Being president of NASPL was a further humiliation. At first he thought reason would prevail and he would be reinstated in his job. He stalled for a while but eventually had to suffer the embarrassment of leaving that position too.

After exhausting all administrative remedies, Blaine appealed his termination to the Superior Court under the Connecticut Statutes of the Uniform Administrative Procedure Act. Judge Samuel Freed ruled in Blaine's favor that he had a "contested case" as defined in the Connecticut General Statutes. That was November 1989.

After nearly two years, another Superior Court Judge, Raymond Norko, was supposed to hear Blaine's request for reinstatement and financial damages. Instead, he revisited Judge Freed's decision that Blaine had a "contested case". There was no new evidence or changes in the law since the first ruling. Normally, Superior Court Judges do not revisit prior rulings of another Superior Court Judge for the same case.

During the proceedings Judge Norko commented that Blaine was smart and clever and suggested that Blaine could have told the Board he didn't like it but he was going to do it because he had been ordered to present it in a positive way. That would still have been disobeying the order and Blaine still would have been fired.

During the proceedings, Judge Norko asked Assistant Attorney General Richard Sheridan how long the Board had been operating with less than 4 members. At the end of the proceedings Judge Norko asked Sheridan what other actions (besides firing Blaine) the 2 member Board had taken, and to get that information to him. Sheridan agreed. The Court had convened to consider Blaine's request for damages and reinstatement. To us, the concern for other Board actions at that time seemed inappropriate and prejudiced.

Even though Judge Norko admits in his November 1991 decision that Blaine served at the pleasure of both the Executive Director and the Gaming Policy Board, he then based his decision against Blaine on the thought that the Statute does not specifically state that both Executive Director and Board must agree to terminate a unit head. It would have been more reasonable for the Court to decide *for* Blaine because the Statute did not specifically state that the Executive Director alone could terminate a unit head.

I believe the pressure, the humiliation and the lack of sleep due to his termination all had a part in Blaine's heart attack and cerebral hemorrhage in May 1992. He was in the hospital for 6 weeks and his left side was paralyzed. His determination and effort were heroic, but the legal case was always on his mind. Even in the hospital strangers recognized him and expressed their support for his work at the lottery and sympathy for the raw deal he had received.

Fighting to regain his health was a lot more difficult with his case still pending. I felt the termination and his treatment by the defendants had contributed, if not caused his heart attack and stroke, and now they were making his recovery and life unbelievably difficult.

The appeal to the Connecticut Supreme Court was heard in October 1992. One would expect the Judges to play devil's advocate, but in this writer's opinion Judge Borden's behavior was rude and unconscionable. He continually interrupted Blaine's counsel. It is interesting to note that Governor William O'Neill had appointed Judge Borden to the Connecticut Supreme Court after Blaine had been fired.

The Connecticut Supreme Court had previously stated that all that was required was that a hearing (Loudermill) be required by regulation. That was sufficient. In Blaine's case they referred to the earlier rulings as dicta and said they did not have to be consistent.

For Blaine's case the definition was changed and the hearing now had to be required by statute rather than regulation. (Personnel Procedure #1 was the state regulation complying with federal law.)

Adding insult to injury, part of the definition of a "contested case" was one requiring a hearing or one "in which a hearing is, in fact, held". Well, there had been a hearing and a hearing was, in fact, held and the Connecticut Supreme Court ignored that too. Judge Freed had not. What was even more infuriating was their total disregard for all the violations of State Law and Statutes that were cited by Blaine's attorney. They took the incredible path of simply ignoring them as well as Blaine's right of free speech under both the Connecticut Constitution and the U.S. Constitution.

Many pages were spent in an attempt to justify the revisiting of the case in Superior Court by Judge Norko. The Connecticut Supreme Court decision was released in February 1993. Almost 4 years had passed in which Blaine had not collected a pension that was due him. He was also owed just short of $47,000 for vacation pay, sick pay, and longevity pay. Now that his Administrative appeal had been exhausted, he requested these funds. He had not been able to request these funds earlier since acceptance of these funds would have constituted a waiver of his right to seek an Administrative appeal with the state.

The state did start pension payments in March 1993, but refused to reimburse him for the missing pension payments from June 1989 to March 1993. They also refused to pay him the vacation, sick and longevity pay owed him. They cited rules that payments must have been made in the month following an employee's departure from state service. They ignored the fact that those payments, at that time, would have constituted a waiver of which they undoubtedly would have taken advantage.

Having exhausted all state appeals, Blaine was now able to take his case to the United States Federal District Court. His suit was for a violation of his freedom of speech as well as for wrongful termination. The state cannot be sued without giving its permission and the Judiciary Committee of the state legislature blocked his request. Therefore his action was against the three state officials directly responsible for firing him. They were Hickey, Cowen and Lange. They were defended by the Attorney General's office.

Two days after the horrendous Connecticut Supreme Court decision Blaine began having seizures. The different medications tried and the medication side-affects made his next two years even more difficult. By early 1995, he had his seizures under control and had fairly good use of his left side. In June 1995 Blaine had another stroke that robbed him of his speech. Blaine had been the most articulate person that I had personally ever known. It is difficult to describe the pain of watching and helping him learn to speak again. All he could think about was regaining his speech so that he could have his day in federal court. As always, he gave it his very best and never complained, but it was heartbreaking to see what they had done to him.

Blaine had not been able to receive his necessary by-pass surgery in May 1992. While waiting for surgery he had suffered a cerebral hemorrhage which made the surgery too dangerous. It was now the fall of 1995 and his heart was failing at an alarming rate. A catheterization showed that surgery was urgently needed. Dr. Henry Low performed the by-pass surgery the day before Thanksgiving, and we were so grateful that it went well.

Depression sometimes comes with by-pass surgery, but Blaine's depression was much greater because of his struggle to regain his speech, an effort made greater by his frustration that he would not be able to express himself well enough in court to receive the justice he deserved. The 1995 speech stroke left him with a problem called "word finding". He would know the word when he heard it, but it was often difficult to think of the name of the person or word on his own. We worked on his speech for 1 to 3 hours each day and his improvement did ensure that he would be able to have his day in court.

In 1995, Blaine and I had been married 40 years, and I had never seen him so upset as when he told me he had worked since he was 17, and this was the first time he had ever been fired. The emotional distress from the unjust firing and the emotional and physical distress from his heart attack and strokes, which I feel would not have happened but for the firing, were an unfair price to pay for his integrity and good service to the state. He should have been retired and enjoying life instead of the hell of the previous 6 years.

I almost lost Blaine again in May 1996. He was hospitalized with heart failure, and while in the hospital he picked up a urinary tract infection. After two weeks he came home thin and weak, and he had to struggle again to regain his health.

Blaine's case was finally scheduled for trial in December 1996 in Federal District Court in Hartford. Bill Rogers had done a fantastic job preparing for the case. Between the records that Blaine had, public documents and what he got under freedom of information, Bill worked for years putting together a solid case with exhibits to back up his every charge and issue. A very capable associate, Bill Champlin, joined him in the trial. Blaine and I never ceased to be astonished at all the effort that went into the case.

One essential witness had to be William T. Drakeley. As Deputy Executive Director, he had been present and had taken notes of all the meetings from May 15 to May 18, 1989. From the day of the order to present the change in Lotto in a "positive" manner, to the day when Hickey put Blaine on leave,

Drakeley was the only person who had always been present. Blaine liked and respected Drakeley and felt he would tell the truth. He feared that Hickey would lie in order to protect himself from an illegal action. Blaine was right and he and Rogers did not want it to be only Blaine's word against Hickey's. Drakeley was the answer. Rogers had taken a deposition of Drakeley in January 1994. Interestingly enough, at that time Assistant Attorney General Sheridan was present, representing Drakeley. Sheridan later represented Hickey, Cowen and Lange at trial.

A requirement for another witness was someone who had worked closely with Blaine on his lottery staff and had held a position of responsibility. Blaine had always felt proud of his staff and felt he could rely on them to tell the truth about his behavior and attitudes at work. He was adamant, however, about jeopardizing anyone's employment, and he felt there would be retribution for anyone still employed by the state who dared testify for him. Gennaro Tursi had been the supervisor of the distribution center for lottery tickets. It was a very important job with a great deal of responsibility. Blaine's job was made easier by the confidence and respect he had for Tursi. They always had got on well at work. Because they had not been social friends, they had not been in touch since Blaine was fired, 7 years earlier. While preparing for the trial, Blaine learned that Tursi had retired from his job with the lottery. Blaine would not have to worry about Tursi losing his job and decided to ask him to be a witness. His response was heartwarming and Blaine was always grateful that he immediately agreed despite the fact that he had moved out of state. Blaine and I were appreciative of the time and effort it required and after so many difficult years Blaine was truly touched when he saw Tursi at the trial.

Choosing witnesses to testify about the effects on Blaine of his being fired and the manner in which it was done was the next step. Not only because we had been married 41 years at that time, but also because he always had shared his problems and work activities with me, I had lived with him through the nightmare of the state courts, and I also had been his care-giver for the previous 4 years, I was certainly a very knowledgeable source. I was nervous about testifying, but I did it with all my heart.

Being his wife might not make me credible with some. We decided to ask a friend of many years who had visited with us frequently before and during the years of turmoil to be a witness and testify to his observations of Blaine. Blaine and I were very grateful to Gerald Atkinson for his willingness to be a witness and for the time and effort it required.

The most difficult decision for me was having Blaine testify on his own behalf. I was terrified that it might cause another heart attack or another stroke. He had waited so long for this trial and he was so determined to do it that we decided to consult with his cardiologist, Dr. Henry Cabin, and neurologist, Dr. Susan Spencer. They both felt that his desire was so great that it would be better to let him testify as long as he had the protection of extra medication to which they both agreed.

Blaine needed an expert on determining his financial losses and for this we depended on Blaine's attorneys. We had never met Dr. Richard S. Martin before this, but we were truly impressed with his credentials. He received his bachelors degree in economics from Harvard, graduate degrees at Cornell, with a Master of Science degree in personnel administration and collective bargaining, and a Doctor of Philosophy degree in economics. He had been a professor of economics at the University of Massachusetts and then at the University of Hartford, he had been a visiting professor at many colleges including Smith, he had written many books, he had done consulting for many large corporations, and he had been active in public service on several boards. We found all the documents that he needed, such as pay stubs and copies of our tax returns and felt assured of his competence.

One of our biggest dilemmas was what to do with the many violations of state statutes and regulations. Blaine had been wrongfully terminated and his freedom of speech under the Constitution had been clearly violated. These were issues that were straightforward and easy to comprehend. The U.S. Supreme Court has ruled that reasonably competent public officials are presumed to know the law under which they operate. It is doubtful that Hickey, Cowen and Lange would claim that they were not reasonably competent.

There was the fear that bringing in the violations of state statutes and regulations would extend and complicate the trial unnecessarily. The Attorney General's office would try to create the impression that Blaine had already lost his case in the state courts and it would be a cumbersome matter to explain how his case had not been tried or ruled on at all, but rather that he had been unjustly denied the right of an administrative appeal.

Furthermore, the Attorney General's opinion that had been written by Sheridan and signed by acting Attorney General Clarine Nardi Riddle concerning the ability of the Board to take action would be depicted as law rather than what it was, an opinion. The Legislature had been very careful in writing Connecticut's gaming statutes to require a quorum of four members of the Gaming Policy Board to take any action. This unbelievable opinion delivered two weeks before Hickey ordered Blaine to lie, stated that only 3 members were necessary, and then in a foot note extended the three down to two Board members. Cowen and Lange knew when they voted to fire Blaine that it was only an advisory opinion and they had the option of not accepting it. Being reasonably competent, they certainly knew the opinion was wrong. They simply used it as an excuse for doing what they wanted. Blaine suffering the consequences as a result was certainly unjust.

I remember the discussion about the state statutes and regulations as Blaine and I, along with his two attorneys went back to their offices. We wanted to be practical and Blaine's attorneys favored the streamlining of the case. It was painful to drop charges of blatant disregard for state laws, and after working so very hard on those very charges, Bill Rogers had mixed emotions. Blaine had confidence in his attorneys and did not want to go against their advice. Even in dropping the state charges, the trial lasted five days.

Lawyers in the Attorney General's office represented the defendants. Their efforts to twist the truth and rattle Blaine and his witnesses were in vain. Blaine was on the witness stand for a whole day, and though my heart pounded harder than I knew was possible, I was so incredibly proud of him, knowing the determination and hard work that had made it possible. The testimony at trial and the many exhibits entered into the trial record clearly proved the injustice Blaine had endured. Cowen demanded to see his earlier deposition when at first his testimony was a total contradiction to that deposition. When later he was told that his testimony contradicted the deposition, he politely asked to see it. After several more rounds, he sat back in the chair, put his hands is front of his face with his palms out in a defensive gesture and said he did not need to see it. It took much prodding from Blaine's counsel but Cowen finally conceded that a refusal to misrepresent something was the same as wanting to represent something only in an accurate way.

The trial lasted the better part of a week during which the jury of 8 always remained attentive. Even the Assistant Attorney General complemented the jury on how exemplary and attentive it had been. The jury deliberated during a period of three days. We wanted to be right there when they announced their decision, so we waited anxiously in the courtroom. The anxiety was heightened by the fact that the jurors had always retained a serious demeanor and we had no idea how the testimony had affected them. When the jury returned to the courtroom and announced their decision, we were overjoyed.

The jury unanimously ruled that Hickey had violated Blaine's freedom of speech and that Hickey, Cowen, and Lange had wrongfully terminated him. Compensatory and Punitive damages were based on expert, detailed testimony. The judgement, including attorney's fees, was a total of $2,048,853. A note from the jury requested that the Court notify NASPL of Blaine's wrongful termination. The judge noted that in his seventeen years on the bench, this was a first. We were truly touched that the jury had understood Blaine's humiliation and the injustice he had endured.

We felt so grateful to the 8 jurors who gave so much time, were so attentive, and were so conscientious in their deliberations. We felt so grateful to Judge Thomas P. Smith for enabling Blaine to have a fair trial.

It had taken seven and a half years to receive the justice and vindication Blaine deserved. Blaine was overcome with emotion. We were also happy for Blaine's legal team, especially Bill Rogers, who had worked so hard and had been so conscientious those many years. It was Blaine's confidence in Bill, and in Bill's integrity and intelligence that were responsible in no small part for Blaine making it through those long, difficult years.

The justice was stolen; the judgement was never paid. The Attorney General's office with its large staff of lawyers, all at taxpayer's expense, was determined to extend the battle to deny Blaine his victory. After an appeal to the District Court was rejected, the Attorney General as counsel for the defendants appealed Blaine's judgement to the 2nd Circuit Court of Appeals. The appeal and briefs were filled with crucial errors unsupported by any evidence and completely contrary to both testimony and evidence entered at trial.[14] It was these very errors that were the basis of the 2nd Circuit's reversal,[15] despite the fact that Blaine's reply brief carefully pointed out the errors with their lack of evidence. It was unfathomable for the 2nd Circuit to accept lies without any evidence and errors that contradicted the trial record. That was January 1999, almost 10 years after Blaine's termination.

Despite the fact that our attorneys told us that the United States Supreme Court only considered approximately 2% of the cases sent to it on appeal, Blaine did appeal believing he would ultimately receive justice. The defendants, represented by the Attorney General's office, repeated the same errors[16] in their reply brief that they had gotten away with at the 2nd Circuit Court of Appeals. Blaine still held out hope for justice and that hope helped sustain us through 1999.

In January 1999 I discovered I had breast cancer and that it had spread to the lymph nodes. Continuing to be the caregiver was a challenge, and now Blaine had to help support me as I went through chemotherapy, surgery, and radiation. I will always be grateful to my surgeon, Dr. Elizabeth Brady and my oncologist, Dr. Patricia DeFusco for their understanding and good care. It was a difficult year but the hope that I would beat the cancer and that Blaine would have his case accepted by the U.S. Supreme Court kept us going.

I was grateful that I was still here for him when the final injustice came in October 1999. The Court denied his petition and it was a bitter blow. Blaine's basic First Amendment Right of Freedom of Speech had been violated and the state got away with it. They also got away with many violations of State Statutes and Regulations, none of which were ever adjudicated. They got away with not paying him any pension for four years, as well as his vacation and sick pay owed him since June 1989. In early 2000, they offered to pay him his vacation pay that they now admitted was owed him, but only if he would sign a waiver saying he was not owed the pension or sick pay. Blaine, true to his character, refused. Several months later, in July, while he was in the hospital, the state sent him a check to compensate him for the vacation pay owed him since 1989, but only that, and with no interest.

The message to all state managers is loud and clear: Play ball, lie when so ordered, the public trust be damned, or otherwise, lose your job. Blaine and I came to the conclusion that Blaine never had a chance against a giant corporation with a large state contract and their influence on state politicians. It was a great injustice to Blaine, but the loss of revenues was an injustice to the state as well. The precedent is an even greater injustice to all state employees and all citizens of this country. The horrendous reversal by the 2nd Circuit Court of Appeals is now case law.

STATE POLICE
INVESTIGATION

On May 9, 1988, the day after General Instrument went on line for the State lottery, two lottery agents were able to select winning tickets after the televised drawing. They reported the errors to the Hartford Courant and then went to lottery headquarters where their tickets were accepted and checks issued. This was only the beginning of the many problems with the integrity of the new system.

This incident was the alleged cause of the State Police report entitled Administrative Investigation, which extended from May 9 to November 9, 1988. It reports the questioning of 23 different people who worked for the state, General Instrument or SNET (Southern New England Telephone Company). Interestingly enough there is no report on questioning the two lottery agents who were the excuse for the investigation. When Blaine met with Jack Burke of the State Police on May 10, 1989, Burke told Blaine that the investigation was done at the request of Orlando Ragazzi, who was then the executive director of the Division of Special Revenue. Ragazzi and the Gaming Policy Board had been in favor of giving GI the 5-year, $40 million contract for the on-line lottery games. Rather than blaming themselves or GI, in our opinion, a phony six-month investigation was launched to see if they could blame Blaine, and all at taxpayer's expense.

Blaine was given a copy of the report on January 10, 1989, after the story had appeared in the press. Where had the report been for the two months since the November 9, 1988 date of the final summary? The thrust of the summary was to blame Blaine's "attitude". In order to reach this conclusion they used incomplete or misleading information, they omitted significant facts, they failed to ask important questions and they failed to interview important witnesses. Blaine responded with examples for each of these abuses.

How Blaine's attitude could explain all the technical difficulties and the need to rebuild all 2200 new GI terminals is incomprehensible. It is interesting however to note who did and did not find fault with Blaine's "attitude", and therefore how much it really meant.

Of the 2 SNET witnesses, neither one found fault with Blaine's "attitude".

Of the six General Instrument witnesses, and one could expect all to blame the lottery chief instead of their own company, five were critical of Blaine's "attitude". One was not.

Of the 15 witnesses employed by the state:
•Eight failed to find fault with Blaine's attitude.
•Four were computer people who had made a one-day trip to General Instrument in Hunt Valley, Maryland and found the risks were no greater to go with GI than any other company. When they could not answer Blaine's specific questions, when their assessment proved wrong, Blaine became a convenient scapegoat.
•One witness from Planning and Research had written a long report, ignoring and never mentioning Blaine's concerns or analysis, and he had highly recommended GI.
•One witness was Blaine's boss who strongly favored GI and was responsible for the investigation. Again, it was easier to find fault with Blaine rather than admit they were wrong.
•One witness found fault with everyone including GI, Gtech (the former vendor), and the Division of Special Revenue's accounting unit. Naturally Blaine, too, was criticized, but he also received praise.

The time spent questioning witnesses was noted in most cases. That average time was close to two hours. The time from an interview to filing a report was inconsistent and varied from 1 to 45 days. Six filings took 30 or more days. Strangely, they were not done in order. What were they hoping for? The summary states that they were looking for a criminal act but found none. Interestingly enough the report was not called a Criminal Investigation. Six months were spent on an "Administrative Investigation" hoping to damage a competent and dedicated employee, truly serious about doing a good job for the citizens of the state.

The following are excerpts of the many faults with the report and summary in Blaine's own words, written at the time the report was released:

"1. INCOMPLETE OR MISLEADING INFORMATION

The ITB (Invitation to bid) was severely criticized and ridiculed. The following facts relating to the ITB were either ignored or minimized by the summary:

A. The draft ITB was circulated to all appropriate unit chiefs at DOSR (Department of Special Revenue) and suggestions and comments were solicited.

B. The second draft was mailed to all potential bidders (including General Instrument) with an invitation to attend a bidders' conference.

C. A bidders' conference was held which was attended by representatives of six potential bidders (including General Instrument). Also in attendance were Deputy Executive Director DOSR, representatives from SNET, DAS (Department of Administrative Services) and interested units at DOSR including some staff members who later criticized the ITB. At this conference the ITB was reviewed page by page and questions were answered. The final version was then sent to DAS for solicitation of bids. Obviously, the attorneys and the technical staff of all six vendors felt that the ITB provided the information necessary for them to understand the requirements and submit a bid. At that time they were satisfied with the ITB. An audio recording and a transcript of this bidders' conference are available.

The report alleges that I and others at DOSR withheld information thereby causing problems for General Instrument:

We refused to disclose the testing scenario we

planned to use in testing the system, much to the consternation of General Instrument. Competent auditors do not tell in advance which accounts they intend to verify. Some information was withheld by the outgoing vendor (Gtech) on the grounds that it was proprietary but this did not include anything necessary for a successful conversion.

The report attempts to place the blame for the serious system problems on my lack of technical competence.

The summary praises the technical competence of the Hunt Valley four but completely ignores mine.

The report attempts to characterize my attitude as poor while ignoring the fact that most of my efforts in connection with the conversion took place in meetings which were audio recorded and the audio cassettes still exist. My assistant handled the day to day activity in connection with the conversion and his attitude was not criticized and he described the communication as "pretty good".

2. BIAS

The summary states "According to Mr. Lewis the state of Connecticut used the 'big bang' approach in 1980 when it converted 480 terminals and must have felt that 2200 terminals could be handled as easily as the smaller system of years ago."

The author of the summary ignored the fact that I told him (p 7 my interview Report) that New Jersey had a "big bang" conversion with 3000 terminals. He also failed to mention that Weslely Hoffman, one of the top technical people at General Instrument was opposed to a phased-in conversion. (p 3 Hoffman interview report). Also omitted was the fact that Ray Sandusky of General Instrument mentioned that New Jersey was "done overnight" (p 2

Sandusky Interview report). Since the author of the summary was present at all three of these interviews, I am forced to the conclusion that these facts were omitted in a deliberate attempt to paint me as naïve.

Conclusions by the author of the summary were often word for word ideas expressed by witnesses who were sympathetic to General Instrument:

"An example of this was Leona Scott of the Licensing and Integrity Assurance Unit who checks the audit reports. When she found mistakes on page 1 of a large report she sent the report back without going on to page 2 to check for errors. When page 2 had an error it went back for corrections without checking page 3. This waste of time...." (p 3 of summary) Also from page 3 of Brian Gorman interview Report. (Gorman was one of the four that went to Hunt Valley)

"This writer has found that the lottery system was built from the bottom or middle up..." (p 7 of summary). Also from page 2 of Brian Gorman interview report

"The words didn't seem to fit the actions or attitude shown later." (p 3 of summary) Also from page 1 of Gary Stein interview report (Vice president at GI)

The summary ignored statements of witnesses that contradicted the statements of witnesses sympathetic to General Instrument: Dan Colarusso (Executive Director of the Information and Technology Unit within the Office of Policy and Management) was asked (p 1 Colarusso telephone interview report) if the ITB specified the SNET lines. When he replied that the ITB spelled out clearly what could be expected from SNET he was then asked if the ITB was vague. "Mr. Colarusso felt that the system was clearly stated as to what SNET would be providing to the vendor of the new system." When this obvious attempt to get a specific criticism of the ITB backfired, this complimentary statement concerning the ITB was omitted from the summary.

3. HEARSAY AND LACK OF PRECISION

"Mr. Hoffman heard third or fourth hand that someone from Gtech was overheard to say that 'It took sometime (sic) for them to find it'…" (p 3 Hoffman interview report.)

"The witness stated that he heard second hand from a staff management team member that Blaine Lewis said he expected them to be cooperative but he didn't expect them to volunteer anything that General Instrument didn't ask for." (p 3 Kirkland interview report)

"…The ITB was requiring the vendor have terminals looking like those now in service…" (P 3 Osswalt interview report) Mr. Osswalt was obviously referring to the ITB requirement that the arrangement of the keys on the new terminal be identical to that of the old terminal. To require the terminals to look like those then in service would have been highly improper and should have been questioned by the investigators.

4. FAILURE TO INTERVIEW IMPORTANT WITNESSES

William T. Drakeley, Deputy Executive Director of DOSR attended the bidders' conference and expressed no dissatisfaction with the ITB. He was also deeply involved as we approached the switchover. He was not interviewed.

Richard Fradette, the CPA who performed the Herculean task of supervising the calculation of the record breaking penalty imposed on General Instrument for system downtime and terminal downtime, was not interviewed.

Lewis Rabinovitz, Esq. who participated in the lengthy and

arduous contract writing sessions with General Instrument, and who could have shed light on the adequacy of the ITB and on my technical competence and attitude was not interviewed.

Beth Reynolds, who is a lottery liaison officer, as is Barbara Porto, and who may not share all of Ms. Porto's opinions was not interviewed.

Even though the investigators claimed to be looking for evidence of criminal sabatoge (p 7 of summary) they did not interview one employee of the outgoing vendor (Gtech) involved in this conversion.

5. FAILURE TO ASK OBVIOUSLY IMPORTANT QUESTIONS

Since the Hunt Valley Four evaluated no vendor except General Instrument, how could they determine and state that the risk factor was no greater with General Instrument than any other vendor? (Exhibit B – p3 under "conclusion" of their report dated 11/24/87)

Why was the Hunt Valley Four not asked the question which I asked in my memo of December 4, 1987 (Exhibit C)? That question being "approximately, what percentage of that information was independently verified and what percentage was taken at face value from General Instrument?"

Why was Edward Osswalt not asked why he did not include my opinions in his memo of December 16, 1987 Exhibit F) even though I requested that the investigators ask this question?

The report notes that Russ Pessina of General Instrument "stated that he sensed a change in J. Blaine Lewis' attitude between 7/29/87 and the trip to the New York factory of Momentum Manufacturing and it wasn't until later that he found out that after the Missouri trip, Mr. Lewis met with Guy Snowden of Gtech in his office. Mr. Snowden is the chairman and chief executive officer of Gtech Corporation." (P 2 Pessina interview report) There is a suggestion here of something dark and sinister. Mr. Pessina was not asked to elaborate, Mr. Snowden was not interviewed, nor was I asked about this alleged meeting. Apparently it was intended that this innuendo just "sit there" and sully my reputation.

6. OMMISSION OF SIGNIFICANT FACTS

The record-breaking penalty of $1.76 million imposed on General Instrument for system downtime and terminal downtime

The discovery by General Instrument that all 2200 sales terminals required rebuilding. (Both of these events occurred before the report was completed and are obviously more important than some of the minutiae included in the report.)

Interview reports of Pardo and Rodriguez who brought the incident of past posted tickets to the attention of the Division were omitted from the report even though this incident was supposedly the reason for the investigation.

I was severely criticized for not protecting General Instrument in the media even though I had protected the previous vendor in 1985. (P 5 of summary, P 5 Osswalt interview report, P 2 Stein interview report) The following was omitted from the report:

Even though General Instrument's problems were far more severe than the incident with Gtech which lasted only a few hours, I defended General Instrument more vigorously than I did Gtech. The following public statements were made by me after General Instrument had been down for a whole day, had sold tickets for a drawing after the drawing, and had hundreds of terminals down even when the system was operating: "I am concerned and really worried." But Lewis said he is "not bashing the vendor". He said the switch to the higher capacity system was a "Herculean" task which was 'a little different than putting a new battery in a flash-

light' and expecting it to work correctly right away."
(Published reports, May 11, 1988)

"Lewis said that despite all the problems no records
of sales or other information have been lost." (Published
reports, May 13, 1988)

Media pressure increased. I was asked point blank on live
radio whether or not I had recommended this change of vendors. I admitted that I had recommended against this change,
my December 4, 1987 memo was obtained under Freedom of
Information and I could no longer defend General Instrument.
"Lottery Chief says that he would replace contractor" did not
appear in published reports until May 14, 1988, five days after
the catastrophe.

My most serious complaint about this report is the apparent obsession with my attitude. It seems to me that the citizens
of Connecticut would be better served if the resources used to
perceive and analyze the attitude of the lottery chief were uti-
lized in investigating the concerns expressed by him about this
contract award and his concerns about the no-bid General Instrument OTB (Off Track Betting) contracts and related trans-
actions of the Division of Special Revenue."

J. Blaine Lewis, Jr. Jan. 11, 1989

The Off-Track Betting contract had not gone to bid for 16
years and Joseph Lieberman, who was Attorney General of the
state of Connecticut at that time gave the opinion that this exception to State Law was legal due to the complexity of the system. It was Blaine's opinion that the on-line lottery system was
just as complex, and he was suspicious of the relationship between General Instrument and the state of Connecticut.

That suspicion was reinforced when the state awarded the
on-line lottery contract to GI, when the state stood by GI despite the contract legally allowing GI to be replaced, and when
the following year he was fired for refusing to lie and advocate
the change that GI had recommended in the lotto game. He had

been willing to give the pros and cons of such a change, he was willing to implement the change if approved by the political policymakers, but he refused a direct order to lie. The change was made and Blaine was fired. Blaine not only had integrity, but his judgement proved correct.

It is interesting to note that three years later, in 1992, the state finally fired their OTB contractor, Am-Tote (a subsidiary of General Instrument). Quoting published reports, "—the state fired Am-Tote, its old OTB contractor, which officials said had been gouging the state."

It is also interesting to note that Brian Gorman (one of the four who made the trip to Hunt Valley and was critical of Blaine) worked at the Division as a consultant and was president of Micro-Tech Computer Services, Inc. His bad judgement was rewarded with further lucrative consulting work for himself and his company for years thereafter.

To analyze what happened to Lotto sales, fiscal 1987-88 was used as a base year, even though sales were less than they should have been due to the GI system-wide breakdown. Sales and net revenues had risen in every year through the 1987-88 fiscal year. Assuming, conservatively, that sales simply stayed the same and stopped growing, the total loss in Lotto sales to and including fiscal year 1994-95 was $382,628,795. This meant a loss in net revenue to the state of $193,450,000. [17]

Lotto sales never recovered from the damage resulting from 6 of 40 to 6 of 44, the change that Blaine refused to recommend. Since 1995 sales have dropped even more drastically resulting in even greater losses in revenues to the state. As of November 1999, sales figures show the state was losing approximately $96,000,000 in revenue every year. Cash 5 was added in 1992 and Powerball was added in 1995. Games are added to increase total sales, not take sales from existing games, but even if the sales had been stolen from Lotto and the sales from these two games were added to Lotto sales, the yearly revenue loss would still be approximately $58,000,000. Making Lotto almost twice as difficult to win killed sales, just as Blaine had predicted. The attempt to blame the design of the Lotto game that Blaine had designed for GI's catastrophic problems had backfired. Ironically, even though the 6 of 44 lotto game has been renamed "Classic Lotto", Lotto players have not been fooled.

BUREAUCRATIC REPORTS

The Division of Special Revenue had taken action contrary to Blaine's recommendations in the past. Awarding the contract to GI was the most recent example. There was no need for him to lie. His recommendation was not necessary. When he was ordered to lie, he refused. He offered to present both pros and cons of a change in the lotto game, to design the game and to implement the game, but he was not going to misrepresent himself in public before the Gaming Policy Board. His boss, William Hickey who had ordered him to lie, had been appointed Executive Director two weeks earlier by Governor William O'Neill. Blaine was fired May 26,1989 for disobeying an order, and he decided he would seek an Administrative Appeal.

Only when Blaine's attorney received material from the Division of Special Revenue under Freedom of Information did Blaine learn of two reports he had never seen. He had responded to the earlier undated, unsigned report entitled "Lotto Lottery Sales Trends" with its constant reference to "declining growth rate'. Both reports that he should have seen, but never did, came from George F. Wandrak, Assistant Unit Head for the Planning and Research Unit.

The first report was titled "Features of Lotto Game Design" and was dated January 10, 1989 (the day after the phony State Police Administrative Investigation hit the press). It was obvious that Wandrak was making a case for changing the lotto game. Here are a few examples of the bias and errors used to support that case: (Bias and errors that Blaine would surely have pointed out had the reports not been hidden from him)

ERRORS

The chart on page 11 lists Rhode Island's game as 6 of 40.

It was 5 of 40.

The chart on page 12, which has numerous statistics for states surrounding Connecticut, has a column for fiscal year 1988 sales. For Rhode Island the figure listed was $78.2 million. $78.2 million was the sales total for 11 months for *Washington DC, Kansas, Iowa, Missouri, Oregon, West Virginia AND Rhode Island.* Sales for Rhode Island for both the 5 of 40 lotto game plus the multistate Lotto America game were only $16.3 million.

BIAS

Per capita sales are omitted from all the charts in this report both on page 12 dealing with the surrounding states as well as on pages 10 and 11 dealing with all lottery states. Connecticut for fiscal year 1988 was #1 in per capita sales for Lotto in the US. Considering much of the minutiae included in this report, this omission stands out.

Page 7, Paragraph 7B titled Multiple Drawing: "Several states provide two or even three drawings per week......." "Currently, Connecticut has only two...." At the time Wandrak submitted the report only Rhode Island had 3 drawings per week. Pennsylvania had had 3 drawings per week from March 1984 to August 1986, when it changed back to 2 drawings per week.

On Page 8 when listing features of different lotto games, the repetition of the phrase "Connecticut Lotto does not offer this feature" was an obvious attempt to discredit the Connecticut Lotto. Many of the pros and cons that would have explained why Connecticut did not offer a given feature were conveniently omitted.

The second report was dated January 27, 1989 and titled: "History of Revenues from Legalized Gaming and Related Statistics Fiscal Year 1972 to 1988"

The January 27, 1989 report was an overview of all gaming in the state, and included statistics on Connecticut's lottery games, transfers to the General Fund and advertising. Page 17 of this report has a chart titled "Fiscal Year 1987 and 1988 U. S. Lottery Sales".

Fiscal year 1988 ticket sales for all lottery games (including lotto) in Connecticut were $513.9 million. This chart incorrectly listed $500 million. It is interesting to note that this chart was almost identical to the one in the October 15, 1988 "Gaming & Wagering Business" magazine with the same $500 million error and including the identical 3 footnotes. The minor differences were the magazine listed the 26 states plus Washington DC in alphabetical order, and it had an additional column for "% change over 87 sales".

The major difference was the omission of the column for per capita revenue for all lottery games that showed Connecticut ranked # 2 despite the fiasco in the 4th quarter with General Instrument (Maryland was # 1).

The chart did show Connecticut ranked # 4 for total lottery per capita sales, but one wonders why the # 2 rank for per capita revenue was left out. Did that make Blaine look too good at a time when the policy makers were trying to discredit him?

These two reports had January 1989 dates. Blaine was lottery chief until May 26, 1989. Why was he not shown the reports for his comments or input? Clearly, every attempt was made to discredit him. His concerns for the lottery and the public interest were getting in the way of the political policy makers.

How ironic that Blaine was fired for his character and excellent service to the state of Connecticut, and George Wandrak received promotions becoming Executive Director of the Division of Special Revenue and eventually becoming president of the Connecticut Lottery Corporation. Blaine's judgement had been correct, but that did not matter. Blaine and the taxpayers of the state were the losers.

Blaine was always a perfect gentleman and never mean-spirited. I thought of that the day of his funeral on December 1, 2000, when George Wandrak came and told me he did not think I would remember him. I told him simply that I did remember meeting him and I thanked him for coming. The dignity of the occasion and my thoughts of Blaine stopped me from expressing my thoughts. Why did he come? Was his conscience bothering him or was he merely curious to see what would be said of the man he had figuratively stabbed in the back?

STATEMENT TO GPB

BLAINE'S PREPARED STATEMENT
FOR GAMING POLICY BOARD

I came to the lottery as an experienced business man, a graduate electrical engineer and a registered professional engineer. I was half owner of a small, very successful manufacturing company. We specialized in electrical and electromechanical products. We sold our computer products to such prestigious companies as IBM and Bell Laboratories. I hold a patent on an industrial analog computer.

In 1973 I was hired by the lottery director to fill the position of assistant lottery director. I served in that position until 1980 when he resigned. At that time I was appointed lottery chief.

During my tenure as lottery chief sales nearly quadrupled. Fiscal year 87-88 was our eleventh consecutive record breaking year. We are now equivalent in net revenue production to #154 on the fortune 500 list. Our lottery has become #2 in per capita revenue production in the United States.

While our lottery was growing, I was also growing professionally and have become an internationally recognized lottery expert. I am serving as president of the North American Association of State and Provincial Lotteries which represents all of the lotteries in the United States and Canada.

I have served faithfully for nearly 16 years and have always followed orders even when I considered them to be extremely unwise and distasteful. I cite the following three examples:

#1 In 1987 I recommended against changing the on-line lottery vendor because I believed that the low bidder was not qualified and responsible. My recommendation was not accepted. I was ordered to change vendors. I did not refuse to comply even though I thought that this was a very unwise decision.

#2 In early May of 1988 I recommended that the new vendor not be permitted to begin operation on the scheduled date of May 8, because in my opinion the system was not ready. My recommendation was not accepted. I was ordered to permit the new vendor to begin operation on May 8. I did not refuse to comply even though I thought this was a very unwise decision.

#3 The new on-line system went live on May 8 and proved to be a disaster. We imposed a record breaking penalty of $1.76 million on the new vendor. It was necessary for the new vendor to rebuild all of the 2200 lottery sales terminals. This terminal rebuilding program was not completed until April 1989. On May 18,1988, because I publicly criticized the new on-line vendor I was ordered to discontinue communication with the news media even though I had been the official lottery spokesman for 8 years and even though this order violated my constitutional rights. Obeying this order put me in the awkward position (as president of NASPL) of being able to speak for every lottery in the United States and Canada except for my own.

Exactly one year later, on May 18, 1989, I have been given an order with which I cannot in good conscience comply. This order requires me to implement a 6/44 lotto game to replace our current 6/40 game. Implicit in this order is the requirement to present this game to the Gaming Policy Board and solicit its approval. Since I obviously would not solicit approval for a game that I did not recommend, there is implicit in the order the requirement to recommend the game. In addition to this implicit requirement to recommend the game I was also given specific oral instructions to present the game to the board in "a positive manner". Since I do not favor changing the game at this time I was placed in the position where I must either disobey an order or misrepresent the facts to the gaming policy board and to the citizens of Connecticut. I chose the former option.

I am not opposed to changing the game when there are indications that it should be changed. Our present lotto game, which for the last several years has been either #1 or #2 in per capita sales in the United States, depending on when you look, is actually our third version of the game.

There is much more involved with the design of a successful lotto game than making it more difficult to win. The size of the field must be chosen with great care. It is tempting to flirt with the idea of using a larger field of numbers which makes it more difficult to win. The best case scenario will produce more rollovers which will result in larger jackpots which will produce sales increases. The best case scenario does not necessarily occur. The worst case scenario goes this way: The field is made larger making it more difficult to win. Customers become angry, sales drop, no one wins, sales drop more and the game is finally scrapped. This is not a wild theory. It has happened.

A very important factor in determining the proper size field is the population. A field size which is suitable for California with 27 million people would obviously be inappropriate for Delaware with a population of 633 thousand. It may be enlightening to examine existing lotto games by comparing the probability of matching 6 numbers with the population. A useful indicator is the ratio of the number of combinations available divided by the population. This could be called the ratio of aggressiveness. For example the ratio of aggressiveness of our current lotto game is 3.8 million divided by 3.2 million which is equal to 1.19. Of all the successful lotto games in the United States there are only two which are higher. For the Florida lotto game the ratio is 1.20 and for New Jersey it is 1.23. One of Massachusetts lotto games, Mass. Millions, has a ratio of 1.62 and this game has produced disappointing results. The 6/44 game which is being proposed would have a ratio of 2.21. This is 36% higher than the disappointing Mass. game. This frightens me. No one knows for sure whether or not this game will succeed but in my professional opinion the risk is too great.

Connecticut citizens near the Massachusetts border will of course be able to choose between our new 6/44 game and the 6/36 Megabucks game. Our game will start with a jackpot half the size of the megabucks jackpot and will be approximately 3.7 times more difficult to win. This will make megabucks approximately 7.4 times more attractive.

James Hosker who is the director of the Massachusetts State Lottery, the most successful lottery in the United States, yesterday made the following unsolicited comment: "If you change that game to 6/44 1 will pick up an additional half million dollars per week on the border." I think he is right and that we would have similar bad luck on the other two borders.

Since our present game is so successful and since there is such a great risk involved with the new game, I prefer to heed the advice of my friends in Maine who say: "If it ain't broke—don't fix it."

I have offered to design a new game to be used when it is determined that we have outgrown our present game.

In the past our games have been initiated in the lottery unit and have been responsible for our enviable sales record. The game which I have been ordered to implement has been recommended by the same on-line vendor which caused all of our recent problems.

Information has been made available to me from reliable sources that this vendor with the assistance of it's public relations and lobbying representative has been calling upon newspaper editorial boards to support their game design to replace our very successful existing game. In my professional opinion this is in violation of the spirit if not the letter of the contract. It was also reported that they called upon the Office of Policy and Management without the knowledge or consent of the lottery. Apparently assuming that the proposed new game would be implemented and that it would be very successful, the revenue figure in the Governor's budget was increased to a figure much higher than the existing lotto revenue. It is my professional opinion that this game is so risky that it might produce less revenue than our existing game.

I am willing to obey all lawful orders and I am willing to design a new game and present it in a balanced manner to a duly constituted board. However, because soliciting the approval of the gaming policy board for this proposed 6/44 game implies that I am recommending it and because Mr. Hickey's oral instructions specified that I was to present it in a positive manner I cannot, in good conscience, obey this order. To do so would constitute a misrepresentation of the facts to the Gaming Policy Board and the citizens of the state.

Respectfully-submitted,

J. Blaine Lewis, Jr.
May 26, 1989

TRIAL TRANSCRIPT OUTLINE

UNITED STATES DISTRICT COURT DISTRICT OF
CONNECTICUT

J. BLAINE LEWIS, JR.
Plaintiff,

CIVIL ACTION NO.
291CV 00432
(AVC)

v.

BRUCE D. COWEN, ROLAND H. LANGE,
and WILLIAM V. HICKEY, INDIVIDUALLY,
Defendants.

December 4, 1996: Pages 1-202
Witness: J. Blaine Lewis, Jr.
Direct Examination: Mr. Rogers
Cross Examination: Mr. Sheridan
Redirect Examination: Mr. Rogers

December 5, 1996: Pages 1-205
Witness: Gennaro Tursi
Direct Examination: Mr. Rogers
Cross Examination: Mr. Sheridan
Redirect Examination: Mr. Rogers

Witness: William T. Drakeley
Direct Examination: Mr. Rogers
Cross Examination: Mr. Sheridan
Redirect Examination: Mr. Rogers
Recross Examination: Mr. Sheridan
Redirect Examination: Mr. Rogers

Witness: Dr. Richard S. Martin
Direct Examination: Mr. Champlin
Cross Examination: Mr. Sheridan
Redirect Examination: Mr. Champlin

Witness: Gerald Atkinson
Direct Examination: Mr. Rogers
Cross Examination: Mr. Sheridan
Redirect Examination: Mr. Rogers

Excerpt of Mr. Lange's Deposition Testimony by Plaintiff

Witness: Concettina Lewis
Direct Examination: Mr. Rogers

December 6, 1996: Pages 1-226
Witness: Alan Mazzola
Direct Examination: Mr. Sheridan
Cross Examination: Mr. Rogers
Redirect Examination: Mr. Sheridan
Recross Examination: Mr. Rogers

Witness: William V. Hickey
Direct Examination: Mr. Sheridan
Cross Examination: Mr. Rogers

December 9, 1996: Pages 1-194
Witness: William V. Hickey
Continued Cross Examination: Mr. Rogers
Redirect Examination: Mr. Sheridan
Recross Examination: Mr. Rogers

Excerpt of Mr. Lange's Deposition Testimony by Defendants

Witness: Bruce D. Cowen
Direct Examination: Mr. Sheridan
Cross Examination: Mr. Champlin
Redirect Examination: Mr. Sheridan
Recross Examination: Mr. Champlin

December 10, 1996: Pages 1-85
Closing Arguments: Mr. Rogers
Closing Arguments: Mr. Sheridan
Rebuttal Argument: Mr. Rogers

Jury Charge

TESTIMONY

Alan Mazzola

Alan Mazzola was personnel director of the Division of Special Revenue at the time Blaine was fired. He had been in that position for over two years and only much later, in 1996, did he become Deputy Commissioner of the Department of Administrative Services. He was with DAS when he was a witness for the defense. His testimony, despite himself, reinforced our conviction that Blaine had been set up.

Under direct examination Mazzola testified that he was a "social friend" of Hickey's. Under cross-examination he admitted that he and Hickey were "close friends" only after reading an earlier deposition where he had used those very words. Mazzola testified several times that he had warned Blaine that Blaine would be terminated for disobeying a direct order, but at the time of the warnings he claimed the change in the game had not been yet decided. At that time Blaine had no knowledge or suspicion of any future order. Mazzola testified that the conversations were "spontaneous" and not "purposeful". Blaine remembered that Mazzola wanted to know how he felt about changing the Lotto game, but was positive that Mazzola never warned him that he would be ordered to recommend it or be fired if he refused.

In retrospect it was obvious to Blaine and me that Mazzola was trying to predict Blaine's reaction to an order his "close friend" Hickey might give. Mazzola testified "yes", "absolutely" and "most definitely" to Blaine being "intelligent" "serious about his responsibilities as a unit head" and being a "person of strong integrity and principle".

Blaine was "very strong willed" "—Blaine was opposed to that change. He didn't make any bones about it." It was a no-brainer to predict that Blaine would not follow an order to misrepresent himself. And that's what they counted on.

At first Mazzola staunchly defended Hickey's order and right to terminate Blaine for not following the order. His insistence was consistent with what Blaine and I suspected. Hickey wanted an excuse for firing Blaine and that excuse for termination for not obeying an order originated with Mazzola and Sheridan. Hickey jumped at it. (Richard Sheridan was the Assistant Attorney General assigned to the Division and was the chief counsel representing Hickey, Cowen and Lange at the trial.) Mazzola testified that he was not aware of Blaine's reports and analysis showing the proposed change in the Lotto was unwise, risky, dangerous and wrong and that he was not present when Blaine was ordered to present the change in a favorable way to the Gaming Policy Board. This was not believable considering he was giving his "close friend" personnel advice and being called into their meetings. In answer to the question "If an employee is ordered to say publicly that he favors a certain policy when he adamantly, truthfully opposes that policy, is that an improper order?" Mazzola begrudgingly, after much prodding, testified "That would be an improper order, yes." He caved in on this one but refused to cave in on the open-minded question despite how foolish he appeared.

Mazzola insisted that Hickey was open-minded and had not made up his mind to fire Blaine until after the Loudermill Hearing. (Personnel Procedure #1 says the Loudermill Hearing has to be conducted by an open-minded decision-maker) He held to this testimony despite the following:

Mazzola knew that Hickey had told Drakeley, right after Blaine had been put on leave and had left the building, that he would terminate Blaine if he didn't obey the order. Obviously, Hickey's mind had been made up and even Hickey later testified that he would have fired Blaine without having a Loudermill Hearing.

Mazzola had called the State Office of Labor Relations to see if Hickey could preside at the Loudermill Hearing. Mazzola testified that Bruce Chamberlain told him that Hickey should stress that he was open-minded, but that no one to his knowledge, including Chamberlain had ever interviewed Hickey to determine whether he was in fact open-minded. Mazzola admitted that in his deposition he had said about Chamberlain "I mean, he stressed it because that is one of the precepts that the court sets out". After reading his deposition Mazzola testified he had said "Yeah, that's exactly what it was" to the question "Was that kind of like advice to protect your backside?"

Mazzola could never recall Blaine's willingness to present the Lotto change in a balanced manner with pros and cons despite the fact that Blaine did so at the Loudermill Hearing and again at the Gaming Policy Board meeting with Mazzola present at both. Again, he was not credible.

Mazzola could not remember that at the Loudermill Hearing Blaine's counsel asked whether the matter of termination was on the agenda for the Board meeting the next day. He could not remember Hickey saying no. He did remember calling Blaine's counsel the next morning as the meeting was starting, to tell him the matter was now on the agenda. Again, his memory was quite selective.

William Hickey

William Hickey, who was Executive Director of the Division of Special Revenue when he ordered Blaine to misrepresent himself and then fired him, also gave very revealing testimony despite himself. In describing his employment (December 1996) he testified that he was a gaming regulator for the "Mashantucket Pequot tribal government"(p 121). His choice of words was carefully chosen since he had skirted State law that would have prevented him from working for Foxwoods for one year after he left the Division. He was so nervous on the witness stand that during his testimony he forgot his story line and in subsequent responses referred to Foxwoods Casino. For example: "I now have five and one half years with Foxwoods Casino——" (page 182) and "I have one of the highest classifications in the casino——" (page 185)

Governor William O'Neill appointed Hickey Executive Director on April 26, 1989. On May 1, an opinion written by

Richard Sheridan and signed by the acting Attorney General Clarine Nardi Riddle was given to the Division. It was the opinion disregarding the State Statute requiring a quorum of four for the Board to take any action. On May 15, a little over two weeks that Hickey had been on the new job, he ordered Blaine to misrepresent himself. Three days later on May 18, Blaine was put on paid leave. This was the day that Hickey told his Deputy that he would fire Blaine if he refused to obey the order. (Deputy Director Drakelely's trial testimony p44) By May 26, a Loudermill Hearing and Board meeting had taken place and Blaine was fired. In ten workdays, May 15 to May 26, their plan was executed. Blaine did not learn of the phony Attorney General's opinion until the Loudermill Hearing on May 24.

Hickey's testimony relative to Governor O'Neill strengthened our convictions:

Hickey knew Governor O'Neill "personally". (p122)

Hickey was appointed to the Board in June '87 after he made the request to O'Neill.(p122)

Hickey was made chairman of the Board after he "contacted Governor O'Neill". (p123)

Hickey was appointed Executive Director of the Division after he "contacted the Governor's office and indicated an interest and I did receive the appointment"(p124)

One would have to be naïve not to suspect that Hickey was being an indebted, dutiful, political hack, and one would have to be even more naïve not to suspect that the Governor had some motivation for wanting to accommodate GI's desire to change the Lotto game. At the time of the disastrous awarding of the contract to GI, it was also O'Neill that was governor. It all added up.

Even though Hickey was a "personal friend" of Ragazzi's (the executive Director at the time)(p 129), and Hickey was a member of the Board at the time, he testified that:

When he voted to award the contract to GI, he was not aware of Blaine's opposition or memorandum (p 128 & p 170) or of Faraci's Memorandum from the Department of Administrative Services (p 171)

He was not aware of Blaine's attitude concerning the timing of the switchover (p129) and only learned about it in the newspapers.(p132)

He was not consulted by Ragazzi before the gag order was issued.(p130)

Despite his past membership on the Board, he testified that Blaine was an appointee just as he was as Executive Director.(p135). He was apparently unaware of the State Statutes involved.

Blaine told Hickey in early May that he had paid his own expenses plus used his own vacation time (two vacation days) plus two week-end days to attend the April meeting of the North American Association of State and Provincial Lotteries (NASPL). Despite being president of NASPL, his trip request was refused. Hickey at trial testified "I felt that—I reinstated two vacation days for Mr. Lewis and charged the trip to business because I felt that's what it deserved."(p137) The added two days never appeared on Blaine's pay stubs, either as added vacation days or regular earnings. He was never reimbursed for his expenses. Hickey was attempting to create the impression that he had treated Blaine fairly in May 1989. The jury was not fooled.

Hickey refers to discussions at the Board meetings in the fall of 1988 "seeking input from him as to how he saw the situation and what he would do to remedy the static sales." (p138) Sales in the fall of 1988 were in a free fall, not static, and Hickey surely knew that. Sales figures were part of the information presented at Board meetings, and Hickey, as chairman of the Board, was present at those meetings according to the minutes. Besides, Ragazzi was a "personal friend" and moreover sales were reported in the same newspapers where he allegedly had learned about Blaine's attitude about the switchover.

Hickey claimed that the decision to change Lotto "was almost unanimous" (p141) and only mentions Blaine being opposed. The clear implication was that Blaine was the only unit head opposed to the change. Drakeley testified "Well, not all unit heads would have been involved in the decision.———"(p 51)

Hickey denied any approval of the change to Lotto by Cowen or Lange in their private meetings in mid May. He testified, "That would be totally inappropriate outside of the monthly meeting."(p142) He obviously was not going to admit violating the law. Cowen and Lange both admitted that the three had met and discussed the change and that they were all favorable to the change. Hickey and Cowen did not admit they had agreed to vote for the change. They knew that was illegal. Lange in his deposition taken in November 1993 also said that the three had met in Hickey's office and had agreed to the change. Lange was not present in court and instead portions of his deposition were read. (pp137-158)December 5 and (pp34-56) December 9.

Question: "And you indicated that there was a dialogue among Cowen, Hickey and you that the Board agreed that the change ought to be made and informed Mr. Hickey of that?" Lange's answer: "Yes" (p54)

Even though Cowen and Lange would normally have only come to the Division once a month for the Board meeting, both had many private meetings with Hickey during the month of May. Yet Hickey testified that he did not tell either of the two Board members that he was going to order Blaine to make the change. (p146)

Hickey denied telling Blaine to present the change in a positive way and testified that he did not even use that word until May 18 and then only to have Blaine "go forward in a positive fashion." (p147) Hickey's Deputy, William Drakeley, was present on May 15, May 16, May 17, and May 18 and testified confirming Blaine's testimony that he was being asked to "misrepresent himself", "prostitue himself" and "was being put in a box". (Drakeley's January 1994 deposition and trial testimony (p 43). Drakeley was present at those meeting at Hickey's request, and it backfired.

Hickey continued to rewrite history when he testified that he had not insisted that Blaine keep the order confidential.(p 151) He ordered Blaine to keep it confidential on May 16 and

Blaine followed that order and only spoke out after he was put on leave. Again, Drakeley was a witness, and his deposition and trial testimony corroborated Blaine's testimony.

It is interesting to note that Hickey in his testimony at trial in 1996 was anxious to explain his knowledge of Constitutional rights of free speech, the illegality of private Board member meetings and private agreements, and the illegality of ordering someone to lie. Did he forget his ordering Blaine not to speak out on May 16, 1989 and that Blaine talking publicly as he had done the year before in 1988 (before the gag order) was an abuse to the Board and the Division and would not be tolerated? (Drakeley's deposition, Drakeley's trial testimony (p 45) & Blaine's testimony (p 123).

In response to asking Mazzola to come and participate in the discussions on May 17, Sheridan asked Hickey "Did he give you advice?". Hickey answered "I followed Mr.——Yes.No. I just wanted him to be aware of what was going on.——"(p 154) Hickey caught himself before admitting he was following Mazzola's advice. They were talking about Mazzola. Hickey was asked "And you asked Mr. Mazzola for advice on how to proceed from that point forward, didn't you?" (After Blaine was put on leave) Hickey answered "From that point forward, I totally follow (sic) the advice of the personnel director of the agency, who's Mr. Mazzola; advice from yourself, Mr. Sheridan; advice from Attorney General Charles Overland and Bruce Chamberlain as given to Alan Mazzola."(p154-5)

It is impossible to believe that Hickey was not following their advice from that point backwards as well. But then again Hickey was never believable. He claimed that Blaine and his counsel were not responsive to his questions at the Loudermill Hearing (p 155) but the transcript proves otherwise. He held the Hearing because he was advised to. In his earlier December 1993 deposition taken by Blaine's counsel, Hickey testified he would have terminated Blaine without a Loudermill Hearing. The truth is he didn't care what Blaine said at the Hearing. He had already made up his mind to fire him. That was the purpose of the impossible to follow order, —impossible for anyone with character, and they all knew Blaine had too much character to lie.

Blaine was concerned about the Division's cozy relationship with Amtote (GI's subsidiary) with regard to their 16 year no-bid contract and with regard to the exception made for them that the state could not examine their books. Instead Arthur Andersen was hired to check Amtote's books. Sheridan in questioning Hickey wanted to establish that it had nothing to do with Hickey or the lottery. Hickey gave "No" answers to "Do you know when it started?", "Did you have anything to do with starting it?", "Did the fact that this special arrangement existed have anything to do with you approving that contract in January of 1988 when you were a Gaming Policy Board member?", "Did that have anything to do with your decision to change the Lotto game to 6 in 44?" Hickey's credibility had already vanished.

Hickey was asked "In your opinion, was that a good decision to change the game from 6 in 40 to 6 in 44?" Answer: "I thought it was a very good decision." Sheridan asked, "Do you know if revenues went up or down?" Hickey answered "When we put the game on, I believe we were about 10 percent below the previous year and we ended up about 1 percent behind."(p 163)

Lotto sales for fiscal 1987-88 were $259,347,000 even with the May and June system- wide breakdown. Lotto sales for 1988-89 were hit even harder and were down to $236,011,000. They would have been even lower had sales not recovered in early 1989 when they were breaking records. Lotto was changed in the fall of 1989 to increase sales an estimated $35,000,000 to $55,000,000. Instead sales that had recovered now plunged even further to $232,860,000 for fiscal 1989-90. Hickey's "about one per cent behind" the previous year should have been an embarrassment.

When Blaine was fired Lotto sales had recovered from the on-line disaster and were breaking sales records. Sales went down the drain with their "good decision". By fiscal 1994-95 Lotto was down to $170,456,205.[1] That was a drop of 34% from fiscal 1987-88. Hickey was not willing to admit the disaster resulting from the Lotto change.

Hickey testified that after he left the Division in May 1991: " there had been a number of invasive changes in the operation. Lotto is no longer the flagship of the Lottery Division. The powerball has taken over." The fiscal year 1990-91 sales for Lotto were down to $219,506,000. Sales were still dropping while he was still there and before the "invasive changes" and he had to know it. Powerball was not introduced until 1995 and it did not "take over". Powerball for fiscal 1999-2000 was $56,500,000. Even for the last completed fiscal year 1999-2000, total sales for Lotto plus Powerball plus Cash 5 were only $148,300,000.

Hickey again finds the truth difficult when asked "And the breakdown was in progress still in the summer of 1988, was it not?" He answered "No. I believe that was repaired very quickly. What General Instrument was doing was upscaling the terminals that were in all the convenience stores and gas stations, but the system itself was running well." (p 174-175)

As a member of the Board he was getting all the reports showing substantial problems into the fall of 1988. The terminals were not being "upscaled". Despite being brand new terminals, they needed several modifications to operate satisfactorily. The rebuilding of the terminals was not completed until April of 1989. It is inconceivable that Hickey did not know this at that time. Indicating he could not remember would have been more believable than his defensive, false answers.

Hickey admitted that the new spokesperson for the Division was not hired until after the GI system breakdown. (p 177)

Hickey testified that he did not know that GI's public relations firm was pushing the change in Lotto through the media and the government. (p 179)

Hickey disagreed with Drakeley's and Blaine's testimony that Hickey had ordered Blaine to misrepresent himself, but then came the following incredible exchange: (pp 201-202)

Question: "At that time on May 18th, Mr. Hickey, do you remember Mr. Lewis saying that he could not prostitute himself?"

Hickey: "Yes, he used that expression."

Question: "Do you remember him saying that he was being put into a box?"

Hickey: "He used that phrase. He was also putting me into a box."

Question: "But you had a real easy way out of your box, didn't you?"

Hickey: (No response)

Question: "Did you also recall that Mr. Lewis said to you that he just could not misrepresent and lie about his true analysis and true views on the proposed change? Did he say that to you on May 18th?"

Hickey: "He did and I say again that I would never, ever have anybody lie or misrepresent any fact anywhere, to the Gaming Policy Board or anyplace else. To do so would be to bully and intimidate someone and, in essence, commit a federal crime and I would not do that."

Why did Hickey think that Blaine objected to prostituting himself, being put in a box or misrepresenting himself and lying if that was not what Hickey was asking him to do? Hickey was more concerned with being guilty of a crime than he was about the truth.

Blaine's counsel had to keep repeating the question before he got a definite answer concerning what Blaine said at the Loudermill Hearing: (pp 220-221)

Question: "Mr. Hickey, did not Mr. Lewis say to you that, 'I will prepare and design the change in the Lotto and I will present that change in a balanced manner to a duly constituted Board.' Isn't that what he said?"

Hickey: "As part of a long presentation."

Question: "Mr. Hickey, did he say that?"

Hickey: "He said that as part of a very lengthy"

Question: "He did?"

Hickey: "—presentation which did not address the order."

Question: "He did say it? Is that yes or no?"

Hickey: "Yes, he said it. Yes."

Roland H. Lange

Deposition Testimony used because Lange was not present in court.

Lange testified that he was not aware of Lewis' views on the proposed change of vendors from G-Tech to GI before the selection was made. (p 39) He does not recall getting five copies of a memo from Blaine with his concerns and negative reactions to the possible selection of General Instrument. (p40)

Ragazzi had set up a meeting with Blaine, Lange and himself at Blaine's request. Lange was then chairman of the Board. Blaine explained his serious concerns about GI and gave Lange five copies of a memo, one for each Board member. Lange took the copies and promised Blaine he would report Blaine's and Faraci's concerns to the Board and give each member a copy of the memo. That was the day before the Board meeting and I can remember how relieved Blaine was that evening that the Board would see what a disaster it would be to award the contract to GI and that reason would prevail.

Blaine assumed that Lange was honorable and would do what he had promised. Imagine Blaine's disbelief when there were no negatives or any reference to the memos before the vote.(p41) Following the Board meeting came another disappointment. Ragazzi ordered Blaine not to discuss the contract award.

Lange testified that he did not remember telling Ragazzi and Blaine that he would bring Blaine's concerns to the other Board members. He only remembered a meeting with Ragazzi and Lewis had taken place before the Board acted. (p40) Lange claimed he did not know that Ragazzi had instructed Blaine not to make any statements about his reservations on the selection. (p41) Lange's failure to recollect the five copies was unbelievable. His failure to discuss any of Blaine's and Faraci's objections to GI being awarded the contract was consistent with Blaine being silenced.

Lange described the system-wide breakdown thus: "There were some very temporary shortages of equipment, et cetera, which were corrected quite promptly." (p 42) Lange and Hickey were both rewriting history to protect themselves from the harsh criticism they both deserved.

Lange denied that the gag order imposed on Blaine in May 1988 was a result of Blaine feeling compelled to respond to the press. (p43) He testified that he had nothing to do with it, but that he agreed with it. (p44) Even though he could not recall anyone else at the Division speaking to the press he would not agree that the order was really directed at Blaine. Lange testified that he did not know GI was promoting the change in Lotto. (p47)

Lange testified that the agreement by Hickey, Cowen and Lange to change Lotto was made before Hickey gave Blaine the order. Question: "You knew that before he made the order to Mr. Lewis?" Lange: "Yes, I would say so." (p54)

Without Lange and Cowen agreeing to the change in Lotto, Hickey would not have been able to set Blaine up for the termination. Lange's and Cowen's nasty, interrupting behavior at the May 26 Board meeting, with no discussion before voting to terminate Blaine indicates that the three had agreed on their plan of action.

Bruce D. Cowen

Cowen testified that he did not know that Blaine was not in favor of the change to GI when he voted to approve the contract. (p64) He was not involved with the timing of GI going on-line, (p66) or did he know that Blaine was opposed to going on-line in May 1988. (p 67) Cowen testified that Ragazzi did not ask him permission to issue the gag order or ask if he could. (p67)

Cowen was initially "requested to serve on the Board by the governor, yes, through initially his legal counsel." (p60) (Governor O'Neill in November 1987)

Question: "How did it come about that you became the chairman of the Gaming Policy Board?"

Cowen: "I had a phone call from the governor's office where the governor requested to meet with me and the governor asked me to be chairman of the Gaming Policy Board. I did not solicit that position." (p69) (But he had told the governor he "would be happy to give something back to the state if he found a way that I would be beneficial to the state and to him and the state."(p.59)

Question: "And so the governor asked you to become chairman of the Gaming Policy Board?"

Cowen: "That's correct."

Question: "And when was that? I'm sorry"

Cowen: "I believe it was in –I don't have the exact date.— April of 1989" (p.69)

Approximately two weeks before the plan to fire Blaine was set in motion, May 15, 1989, both Hickey and Cowen were appointed to their new positions: Hickey as Executive Director on April 26, and Cowen as chairman of the GPB to replace Hickey. It is interesting to note that this time the governor wanted to meet with Cowen. One can only wonder what was said or agreed to.

Cowen testified that he did not know GI's opinion about the Lotto change and indicated changing the odds originated with the Board in an attempt to increase state profits. For Board members who had never involved themselves with the operational aspects of the Division, testified to incredible ignorance of what was going on in the Division, and according to Blaine had never been involved in the design of any lottery game (all games had always been designed in the lottery unit), Cowen's testimony was a stretch:

Question: "Prior to April of 1989, had there been discussion at Board meetings about the possibility of changing the Lotto game from a field of 6 in 40 to 6 in 44?"

Cowen: "Sure. The minutes, you can look at the minutes in October, December and January. As Board members we were inquisitive as to how we can maximize revenue to the state and we requested information of the Division, and in this case Mr. Lewis, regarding how to increase revenue and what a potential change in Lotto could mean."

Question: "Do you have any idea where that idea first came from? That is whether or not to change the game?"

Cowen: "Well, we weren't initially looking at making the

change. We were looking at, in our role, is to have a dialogue, to be able to create some discussion. Are there ways to increase the profitability to the state? We were a revenue-generating group. And I believe in October we asked, Do you have any suggestions?"

Question: "Ask who, Mr. Cowen?"

Cowen: "Mr. Lewis. And he felt that the game was fine. We don't need to do anything. And I think later in December, and I think the minutes will reflect, since we really did not receive, you know, any recommendations from his group, we then requested him to present us certain data on what a change would mean if it was 6 in 42, 43, 44, 45, 46 so we could analyze it to see if it made any sense."

Question: "And your testimony is that began in October of '87?"

Cowen: "No. In October of 1988. It could have been sooner than that——" (pp69-70)

Question: "Do you know what the attitude of General Instrument was toward that change?"

Cowen: "No. You know, I have heard about this General Instrument, but I was unaware of any dealings by General Instrument in promoting the change."

Question: "So you don't know if they were in favor or against it?"

Cowen: "During that period from October through January, I never knew that General Instrument had an opinion." (p71)

Cowen testified that the Board did not receive any recommendations from Blaine despite Blaine's four page report to Ragazzi dated October 11, 1988 and his subsequent reports at Board meetings.

The minutes of the October 27, 1988 Board meeting devote 68 lines to covering Blaine's report to the Board, the ongoing problems, his lotto analysis, steps to be taken to overcome the GI problems and answers to questions.

When Blaine told the Board that despite their problems, Connecticut had the 2nd or 3rd best lotto game in the country, Cowen asked what that was based on. Blaine told him it was based on per capita sales from states that had lotto games. Blaine was there to give his analysis based on his sixteen years of lottery experience. Apparently when Cowen testified that he was not getting any recommendations, it meant that Blaine was not telling him what he wanted to hear.

The same minutes devoted 2 lines to the Off Track Betting report, 3 lines to the Licensing & Integrity Assurance report, and 47 lines to the Gambling Regulation report.

The minutes indicate that more time was spent discussing the lottery than all of the other units combined.

The minutes of the December 29, 1988 Board meeting devote a dozen lines or less to reports from each of the following four units: Administration, L&IA, Gambling Regulation and OTB. The same minutes devote 69 lines to the lottery. Cowen knit-picked about the ads from the new advertising agency, Decker, Guertin & Cheyne, that had been chosen by a committee of 7 people, only 2 from the lottery. When Blaine was asked to grade them, he explained he was working with them to improve but he would give them a B or B-. Cowen stated he would only give them a D. Blaine always remained a gentleman, answered questions seriously, and treated Board members with respect.

In response to a battery of questions submitted by the Board, Blaine responded with his January 18, 1989 four and one-half page report.

Blaine's three-page memo dated February 7, 1989[2] gave the history of Connecticut Lotto games and sales as well as Blaine's detailed analysis of how a game is designed. He explained his "booster plan" and steps taken to insure that Connecticut had a successful Lotto game despite its small population.

For Cowen to testify that Blaine had not made any recommendations to improve sales or that he, Cowen, was not aware that GI was pushing for the change from October 1988 to January 1989 is beyond comprehension. Cowen should have been humiliated that he had been proven wrong. Instead he rewrote history.

Cowen testified that he had a meeting early in the morning on May 22, 1989 with Hickey and Lange. That was the day that Blaine came to Hickey's office and received notice of his Loudermill Hearing. (Blaine had been suspended the previous Thursday.) May 22 was a Monday and the Board meeting was scheduled for three days later, May 25. Cowen claimed that he did not know about Hickey's order on May 22 and only found out about it on May 25.(pp72-74) One wonders why Cowen and Lange would make a special trip to the Division on May 22, the same day Blaine was to come in and get notice of the Loudermill Hearing and yet not be told of the order until May 25.(p73) They could not admit to deciding anything. That would be illegal. They certainly did not make the trip to discuss the weather. Cowen contradicted his testimony in his December 1993 deposition:

Deposition testimony:

Question: "Now, you said you had learned that Mr. Hickey was going to order Mr. Lewis to prepare or present the change in the Lotto game prior to the time that Mr. Hickey gave that order to Mr. Lewis; correct?"

Cowen: " I believe so."

That means that Cowen knew about the order before May 15, not on May 25 as he testified in court. In his deposition Cowen also admits that he was advised of the Loudermill Hearing on May 22, before it took place:

Question: "There is no doubt in your mind that you were advised of the –about the Loudermill hearing that was going to take place with regard to Mr. Blaine Lewis, that you were advised of that before it took place? You were advised of that on the 22nd?"

Cowen: "Yes"

Cowen also testified in his deposition that he had a meeting with Hickey between May 22 and May 25: "I believe it would have had to have been May 24th and it regarded Mr. Hickey asking that an item be placed on the agenda for the next day."

Question: "So if your deposition said that, that was truthful testimony at the time that you gave the deposition?"

Cowen: "Yes" (p120)

Cowen testified that there was a meeting with other people, including Hickey and Lange and Sheridan prior to the Board meeting on May 25: (p138-140)

Back to trial testimony:

Question: "I said at the time the meeting started on the 25th who did you expect to make the presentation?"

Cowen: "Mr. Ziemak"

Question: "How did you know that?"

Cowen: "Mr. Hickey informed us."

Cowen: "He informed us the morning of the 25th."

Cowen: "He explained that to us as well as Mr. Sheridan, who was in the meeting before and on the 25th, the Board meeting and the meeting after."

At the May 26 Board meeting when Blaine was fired, Blaine had said about obeying the order: "To do so would constitute a misrepresentation of the facts to the Gaming Policy Board and the citizens of the state."

Cowen admitted that Blaine said he would not misrepresent himself at the May 26 Board meeting but Cowen testified that was not the same as lying. After twenty questions and mostly evasive answers (pp129-132) Cowen was then asked:

Question: "Let me try again. When I say to you I will not misrepresent something, what am I telling you? Isn't it that I will represent it only in an accurate way. I will not misrepresent it? Am I saying that?"

Cowen: " No. I will agree with that."

Cowen's testimony at trial was very frequently a contradiction of his December 1993 deposition. At first he was aggressive about seeing the deposition, not believing his own words. As the cross-examination progressed he became less aggressive and more humble and finally accepted the quotes from his own deposition. Finally, he put his hands in front of his face and backed up in his chair in a defensive manner saying there was no need to see the transcript. Following are examples from the long progression:

(p 108)

Question: "Did you testify previously under oath in answer to the question as to whether or not you knew before Hickey gave the order, 'I believe so'?"

Cowen: "If you- - you haven't shown me the deposition."

Question: "You don't believe me? I will show you the words."

Cowen: "You want me to respond?"

Question: " 'I believe so' And you see those words and you spoke those words, didn't you, sir?"

Cowen: "That's what the deposition says; correct."

Question: "And the deposition says it because you said it under oath; isn't that right?"

Cowen: "That was my memory at that time."

(pp 109-110)

Question: "Did Mr. Hickey tell you around that time on May 17th that Mr. Lewis was resisting the order?"

Cowen: "I don't remember that."

Question: "You don't remember. Well, let me show you your deposition. Maybe that will help. Let me show you your deposition, page 81. I draw your attention to lines 18 to 20. 'Question: Did Mr. Hickey tell you around that time, May 17th that Mr. Lewis was resisting the order?' and your answer at that time, sir under oath, sir, was 'Yes'. Do you remember that now?"

Cowen: "That's what it says"

Question: "And that was your testimony under oath, wasn't it?"

Cowen: "That was my testimony"

Blaine's counsel read from Cowen's deposition again on p 116 and p 119 and p 120 to refresh Cowen's memory.

(pp132-133)

Question: "You would agree with that. Okay. Now, on the 22nd, you were aware that the subject of the Loudermill hearing on the 24th was going to be the possible termination of Mr. Lewis, weren't you?"

Cowen: "I was aware it was a disciplinary action."

Question: "And that possible termination was one of the outcomes, weren't you?"

Cowen: "I don't remember that."

Question: "You don't remember that. Do you see a distinction between termination and separation of permanent employee?"

Cowen: "Well, I think there is, you know, I guess in looking at it—did I use the word 'separation'?"

Question: "Yes"

Cowen: "Maybe it should have been 'suspended.'"

Question: "Your testimony was, 'I knew this was a hearing for a suspension or potentially a separation for a permanent employee.'"

Cowen: "It was a suspension. Can you read it back? Did it say 'suspension'?"

Question: "Well, you know what, you can never depend on the handwritten word because there is always the possibility that you misread it. So let's go to the typed.

Page 85 in your deposition, line 22. Question: 'Well, were you aware at the time when Mr. Hickey told you that he was going to conduct the pre-termination hearing, Loudermill hearing, did you know what that meant at the time?' Answer: 'I knew that this was a hearing for a separation. Pre-termination for potentially a separation of a permanent employee.'"

Cowen: "May I see it?

Question: "Absolutely. Right here at the bottom of line 22 and 23."

Cowen: "Not that I don't trust you."

Blaine's counsel was cross-examining Cowen and putting colored circles on a chalk board showing the days of the calendar of May 1989. Cowen, Hickey and Lange were each represented by a different color and the appropriate color was used to circle the days when any two had met. The phone call was noted with a PH by the circle. The object was to show the many meetings that had taken place coinciding with Hickey's order to Blaine on May 15 to his termination on May 26.

(p 140-141)

Question: "You knew it back on the 18th. We went through that before. That's why your color and Mr. Hickey's color was on the 18th. He told you about the suspension."

Cowen: "I don't remember."

Question: "You don't want me to go back to that?"

Cowen: "I don't remember specifically what day I was told, but I will go along with it."

(pp146-147)

Cowen was chairman of the Board that met on May 26, 1989 to terminate Blaine. At that meeting Hickey spoke with no interruptions for 203 lines (from page 1 to the bottom of page 7) of the transcript.

Question: "Page 7 of the transcript and finally at the bottom of page 7 you say 'Thank you, Mr. Hickey'; right?"

Cowen: "That's correct."

Question: "And actually on the 7th page you ask him if he has anything else he wants to add, don't you?"

Cowen: "That's correct."

Question: "Mr. Lange didn't interrupt him either for seven pages, did he?"

Cowen: "No"

(pp148-152)

Hickey had been allowed to speak for 7 pages, consisting of 203 lines, without interruption. Blaine's counsel with the transcript in hand counted 14 lines before Blaine's first interruption. Cowen interrupted Blaine a second time after another 25 lines (39 lines total). After Blaine explained that he was getting to Hickey's charge,

Lange at that hearing added: "I think you are abusing the privilege that we are offering you."

Continuing to read from the May 26, 1989 script of the hearing,

Cowen said it was "not a media event", and added: "I see four cameras over here and I don't know of any other state employee terminated, or proposed to be terminated, that there would be four cameras from different stations televising it. —"

Question: " And you didn't like it that the press was there, did you?"

Cowen: " I didn't agree. It's not a matter of the did I like or dislike."

Question: "And you also thought that Mr. Lewis, by giving some of the history of his service to the state, was insulting the Board, didn't you?"

Cowen: "No"

Question: "Then why, sir, did you say, 'Then do not insult the Board by giving us history?"

Cowen: "Because what I meant was it wasn't relevant to what the issues were."

Question: "Why did you use the word 'insult'? Why not say it's irrelevant? Why say it's insulting the Board? You felt insulted, didn't you?"

(pp154-155)

Blaine's counsel returned to the transcript and quoted Cowen when he interrupted Blaine in a very sarcastic tone for the third time:

Cowen from transcript: "Mr. Lewis, I thank you for your insight on the change in board size, but that is not the matter before this Board today.—"

When Blaine's counsel made the point that Lewis had not been able to give his views on the Lotto change at the only Board meeting (May 25) where it had been on the table with a proposal, Cowen responded about Blaine:

Cowen: "He didn't elect to attend."

Question: "His views were not heard because he was suspended as head of the Lottery, isn't that right?"

Cowen: "He was not at the meeting and his views were not heard."

Not only was Blaine suspended, but his counsel was not even notified of that May 25 meeting until it had already started. "He didn't elect to attend." was a real disingenuous wise-crack.

(pp156-158)

Blaine's counsel next read part of Blaine's statement from the transcript of the May 26 meeting:

Question: "All right let me read it to you. 'Because Mr.

Hickey's oral instructions specify that I was to present it in a positive manner, I cannot in good conscience obey this order. To do so would represent a misrepresentation of the facts to the Gaming Policy Board and the citizens of the state.' He said that, didn't he?"

Cowen: "Yes."

Question: "Did you ask Mr. Hickey whether, in fact, he had given that order that it be presented in a positive way?"

Cowen: "I had seen a copy of Mr. Hickey's order in writing and I don't remember if I had asked the question on 'positive'."

Question: "And you didn't ask him at the hearing, did you?"

Cowen: "I don't believe so, no."

Question: "And there was the recess at the end of the hearing and that recess lasted an hour, from 4:15 p.m. till 5:12 p.m., just about an hour, isn't that right?"

Cowen: "Correct"

Question: "And then you returned at 5:12 p.m. after the recess and you reconvened the meeting, didn't you?"

Question: "And your first words after reconvening the meeting were, 'Mr. Lange, may I have a resolution, please,' is it?"

Cowen: "That's correct."

Question: "And Mr. Lange immediately said, 'Yes, sir. I'd like to present this motion and resolve that the Gaming Policy Board hereby approves the recommendation of the executive director to terminate the employment of Mr. J. Blaine Lewis,' and then you seconded that, didn't you?"

Cowen: "That's correct."

Question: "And without any discussion at all, you said, 'All those in favor?' and everybody voted in favor, you and Mr. Lange?"

Cowen: "That's correct."

Cowen was obviously fed some numbers to use during his Redirect examination. It was a slick attempt to deceive, but he should have been embarrassed. He testified that there were record lottery sales for 89/90, 90/91, and 91/92. That was due to the additional instant games for which Blaine had planned. In addressing Lotto sales he said:

Cowen: "One of the biggest decreases of Lotto, $100,000,000 and the reason for that was Cash Lotto, which has a bigger jackpot than Lotto, took a lot of the sales away from Lotto and moved them to Cash Lotto. Lottery has been very successful in, I will say, five of the six subsequent years. It states it in the facts. They are in the reports. It speaks for itself." (pp161-162)

Cowen knew or should have known that Cash Lotto was not introduced until 1992, and that the jackpots were not bigger than Lotto.

Cowen knew or should have known that the energy, money, and design of a new game were to add to total sales, not steal sales from an existing game.

Cowen knew or should have known that for its first full year of sales, fiscal 92/93 Cash Lotto sales were $33,289,095 compared to Lotto sales of $202,473,626. The two together were still well under sales for Lotto alone in 87/88

Cowen knew or should have known that despite an increase in total lottery sales, by fiscal 92/93, revenue to the state went down. As a businessman he should have noticed.

In fiscal year 87/88, total lottery sales of $514,597,000 resulted in $225,000,000 to the General Fund.

In fiscal year 92/93, total lottery sales of $552,545,506 resulted in $221,700,000 to the General Fund.

As Lotto continued to decline, the addition of a multitude of instant games and Cash Lotto resulted in decreased revenues, and they no longer compensated for the damage done to Lotto.

But all these numbers are beside the point. Blaine was correct in his analysis of the Lotto change but that is really beside the point. What really matters is that in their rush to fire him, they violated his freedom of speech and treated him in a humiliating fashion. Cowen and Lange were both rude and pompous at the May 26 meeting. Blaine had always been a gentleman and was a gentleman even when receiving their nasty treatment. They violated many state laws and statutes and did not care. They deprived the state of an excellent, competent, honest manager and in so doing hurt state revenues as well.

A brief comment is in order here that addresses the character of two of the defendants. I earlier made reference to Hickey going to work for Foxwoods despite violating the state requirement of a one year wait. He got around that by claiming he was employed by the Mashantucket Pequot tribal government.

Cowen was president and director of TRC, an environmental services firm, and had been in that position in 1989 when he voted to fire Blaine. In April 1997, there were published reports he violated the company's restriction and exercised TRC stock options without authorization from TRC's board. With no public denial, Cowen resigned his position at TRC and reportedly was negotiating a repayment to the firm for the benefits he obtained.

William T. Drakeley

Drakeley had served for several years as the deputy director of the Division and was serving in that capacity when Hickey was executive director. He had been present and had taken notes of Blaine's meetings with Hickey on May 15 through May 18. He had worked with Blaine for several years:

Question: "How would you describe Mr. Lewis's reputation in terms of integrity, honesty and truthfulness?"

Drakeley: "Unimpeachable. He was a dedicated state employee. There was never a question about his integrity or character." (p 36)

Referring to Drakeley's deposition of January 1994:

Question: "Then I asked you, 'By the way, the written order which is dated May 16, which is Plaintiff's exhibit—given by Mr. Hickey to Mr. Lewis, that does not mention anything about positive manner, does it?' And your answer was, 'No, I don't recall that it did.' And then I asked you, 'But that was part of the verbal order that Mr. Hickey gave Mr. Lewis on May 15th' And your answer was 'Yes, it was.' Do you recall that?"

Drakeley: "That's correct; I recall that." (p 42)

(p 43-45)

Question: "And at the meeting on May 18th, did Mr. Hickey say that he refused to withdraw the order?"

Drakeley: "Yes"

Question: "And at that time Mr. Hickey then repeated the verbal order to prepare and present this change in a positive, favorable way; is that your recollection?"

Drakeley: "That's my recollection"

Question: "Now, what did Mr. Lewis say at that point? Do you recall him saying that he felt he was being put in a box?"

Drakeley: "Yes, I recall that."

Question: "And do you recall Mr. Lewis saying that he could not prostitute himself?"

Drakeley: "I recall that word. This is vivid in recollection. It would be helpful—I mean, I took the minutes so I know exactly what was said and I jotted everything down, all the important comments that were made by the parties that were there——"

Question: "Now just to follow on that, so in effect Mr. Lewis at that meeting on May 18th, did he say that he could not do it?"

Drakeley: "That's correct."

Question: "Now, after Mr. Lewis left, you were there and you were there along with Mr. Hickey. Did Mr. Hickey tell you that if Blaine did not obey that order that he would terminate him?"

Drakeley: "At the conclusion of the meeting there was some discussion about the necessary steps that would have to be taken if Mr. Lewis insisted on not carrying out the order."

Question: "At that time Mr. Hickey told you that if Mr. Lewis didn't obey the order he was going to terminate him?"

Drakeley: "Yes"

Question: "Now, also I'd like to go back to the meetings, as you recall them, May 16th, 17th, 18th. Did Mr. Hickey order Lewis not to talk about the order?"

Drakeley: "Yes"

Question: "Did Mr. Hickey also say at that time that he was not going to tolerate any of the same kind of comments or public responses that Mr. Lewis had made during the breakdown in 1988?"

Drakeley: "That's correct."

Question: "and did he say that- - did Mr. Hickey say that he considered those to be an abuse of the Division of Special Revenue and the Gaming Policy Board?"

. Drakeley: "That was his feeling."

Under Recross examination Sheridan asked a question that backfired: (p 63-64)

Question: So when Mr. Hickey told Mr. Lewis to present it in a positive manner and not to talk about it, he wasn't saying you couldn't express your opinion, was he?"

Drakeley: "He was restricting, I think, his public discourse on the topic. —"

Dr. Richard S. Martin

(pp66-77)

Dr. Martin, a retired professor of economics and consulting economist was a witness for Blaine. He received his degrees form Harvard and Cornell. He had taught at the University of Massachusetts in Amherst where he was on the faculty of the Economics Department for ten years. Then he moved to the University of Hartford where he retired from active teaching in 1992, but was still listed as a member of the faculty, professor emeritus. To give his comprehensive background including the firms for which he had done consulting, the studies he was involved with, the books he wrote, the public service on public boards, and a description of what an economist does took eleven pages.

(pp82-83)

When questioned about the information he needed to do his calculations he detailed all the information he received from Blaine and me. To make it perfectly clear he was then asked:

Question: "So when you looked at these materials, you had what we would call private information from the Lewises in the form of their tax returns and private pay stubs and those sorts of things; is that right?"

Martin: "Yes"

Question: "And you also had public information in the form of a state employee manual, the handbook, and various information about the state's pension program?"

Martin: "And fringe benefit programs. The pension, the life insurance and the 401K plan, yes."

(pp85-86)

Question: "You don't do this for free?

Martin: " No"

Question: "And how are you compensated for the time that you spend?"

Martin: "In a case of this sort, it's done on an hourly basis and the current rate is $175.00 an hour."

Question: "And from your personal perspective as a witness, it doesn't matter to you one way or the another (sic) what happens in this case because you were retained as an expert to give your personal opinion?"

Martin: "I was retained to give a professional opinion and before I got involved in this, I had never met the Lewises, didn't know them at all."

Question: "You don't have a provision in your arrangement where you get extra depending on what the jury may award to Mr. Lewis in this case?"

Martin: " No. It's strictly a (sic) time spent."

(pp113-114)

Martin then proceeded to answer and explain exactly how he had arrived at his figures for Blaine's financial losses due to being fired. Sheridan seemed to think that he could catch errors and embarrass Martin, but he failed miserably. Martin answered his questions in great detail and there was even a series of answers that must have been awkward for Sheridan:

Question: "——I'm trying to figure out how you came to that number?"

Martin: "The actual values were taken from - - with regard to vacation pay, were taken from a letter, I believe, from Mr. Mazzola to Mr. Lewis as of the time of termination. The sick pay calculation - -"

Question: "Tell me how you calculated that? Let's take the sick pay. Tell me how you calculated that, please?"

Martin: "I'm sorry. I didn't calculate it. That figure was contained in a letter you wrote to Mr. Lewis under the date of April 12, 1995."

Question: "What about the rest of these figures? Where did you get the rest of these figures?"

Martin: "Well, the $28,000. which is the other part of the figure as of the time of termination, was also contained in your letter dated April 12, 1995. If you add those two figures together, you arrive at the total of $41,359."

Question: "In direct testimony you said you applied a formula?"

Martin: "Yes"

Question: "What you, in effect, did was take my figures. You didn't apply any formula at all?"

Martin: "I applied a formula in terms of arriving at the values of these in February 28, 1992."

Question: "You applied the formula or you took my figures, didn't you?"

Martin: "For as of the time of termination, the numbers are your numbers. As of the time of expected retirement in February of 1992, it's my number."

Gennaro J. Tursi

(pp12-19)

Tursi, now retired, testified that he worked for the lottery as supervisor of the distribution center at the time of Blaine's termination, and had worked for the Division since December 1971. He had known Blaine the whole time Blaine had been employed at the lottery. (That would have been 16 years, working with Blaine.)

Question: "Would you describe, as best you can, your experience with Mr. Lewis in terms of, first of all, his work ethic?"

Tursi: "His work ethic? Exemplary, as far as I'm concerned."

Question: "What was Mr. Lewis's attitude about the lottery? Go ahead."

Tursi: "I think his attitude, as I say, he lived it and thought it was very important and he wanted - - everything he did, he wanted to make sure it was a success and it was, as far as the years I was with him. Every avenue that he took in the lottery, it was a success."

Question: "How about Mr. Lewis's reputation for integrity, what is your observation about that?"

Tursi: "Well, as far as I'm concerned, I think it was unsurpassable, top quality. I think he had the same respect of his other lottery affiliates in the national and like that. He was well-respected there."

Question: "How about his knowledge of the lottery and gaming operations in the Lottery unit?"

Tursi: "Very, very in-depth. He was well-knowledged about lottery, every aspect of it as far as I'm concerned."

Question: "How would you describe his knowledge of the lottery in relation to the other people that he worked with?"

Tursi: "I would dare say he was more knowledgeable about the workings of the lottery than others. I figured he was the expert, as far as I'm concerned, in the lottery."

Question: "In his dealings with his fellow workers in the unit, including you, what kind of attitude did he display?"

Tursi: "Well, like a superior, but he was fair, very fair. He'd listen to us."

Question: "Were there monthly - -excuse me - - were there weekly meetings?"

Tursi: "Staff meetings? Yes, on the weekly basis, staff meetings."

Question: "And how would he conduct those meetings?"

Tursi: "Very well. He would ask us - - he would come up with what he wanted to do and ask us what we thought of it, listen to what we had to say and then made a decision based on the input we gave."

Question: "Was he friendly?"
Tursi: "Yes"
Question: "Did he have a sense of humor?"
Tursi: "Always"

Sheridan in his cross examination attempted to discredit Tursi's testimony with his false assumption that Tursi was helping a social friend. (p 23)

Question: "Gerry, are you a personal friend of Mr. Lewis's?"

Tursi: "Over years I have become a friend of Lewis's."

Question: "Can you explain that to me? How do you mean?"

Tursi: "Friends—well, how do you mean friends?"

Question: "Social?"

Tursi: "No"

Question: "You're not social friends so your relationship was an employer/employee?"

Tursi: "Yes."

After that bad guess, Sheridan tried again.

(pp 26-27)

Question: "He was the expert?"

Tursi: "As far as I'm concerned, yes."

Question: "Do you think he resented somebody having an idea to do with the lottery that didn't originate with him?"

Tursi: "No"

Question: "You don't think so?"

Tursi: "I don't think so."

Question: "You think he was open to that?"

Tursi: "I think so."

Sheridan had tried to discredit Tursi's knowledge of Blaine by having Tursi testify that he worked as supervisor of the distribution center (also called warehouse), a separate building and had staff meetings with Blaine only on a weekly basis.

(p24)

Question: "How often would you see him?"

Tursi: "At least once a week."

Question: "And that was what, an hour?"

Tursi: "Probably a good part of the morning."

In Redirect examination by Blaine's counsel:

(p 32)

Question: "Did he visit you frequently at the warehouse

also?"

Tursi: "He would come visit me."

Question: "So you saw him on occasions other than the staff meetings?"

Tursi: "True."

Question: "And at the warehouse?"

Tursi: "Uh-huh."

Question: "Would you see him outside the warehouse and outside of staff meetings also?"

Tursi: "Very rarely, but I was in constant telephone communication with him. We were on the phone more than I think we saw each other."

Gerald Atkinson

(pp121-135)

Gerry as a long time, good family friend testified that he had known Blaine for approximately 40 years and had seen him often during the time from May 26, 1989 through the present. (pp 121-122) In describing Blaine, Gerry testified:

"Well, judging from conversations over many years, you know, I would have regarded him personally as the complete professional. He came across in what he said to me as very conscientious, very involved.———He talked a lot about his work. He was clearly proud of the lottery and his involvement with it. He had a phrase that he often referred to it as a Fortune 500 company because of its ability to generate big revenues for the state of Connecticut and still operate at a very low overhead.———he was clearly very proud of the lottery and he's also very proud of the people who worked for him. He regarded it as a team operation in which he was a team member. He was very proud of team accomplishments."

Question: "How would you describe Mr. Lewis's attitude, his personality, emotional condition before he was terminated?"

Gerry: "Before he was terminated, I would have described him as very happy, very upbeat, very outgoing. He was confident in the present. He seemed to be optimistic about the future. He was interested in many things; politics at all levels, world affairs, famous people, the construction projects he was doing around his home and he talked about all of these. He had a good sense of humor. He did a lot of singing and laughing.———" (p126)

Question: "Now from your observation, how did Mr. Lewis react to his termination?"

Gerry: "His reactions, to my way of thinking, fell into two phases. The first phase was disbelief, shock, anger. He couldn't believe that someone with his proven track record could have been booted out and in such a humiliating way. So that was his first reaction.

Blaine is a reserved person and can and tends to hide his feelings, but I could see that his firing hit him very hard.

Then the second phase was he sort of gathered his strength and he began to plan for his reinstatement to his previous position, vindication of his professional judgement about the lottery and the restoration of his reputation. And at that time he would frequently say, I will have my day in court. I will have my day in court."(p127)

Question: "How about his conversation after his termination in comparison with the way he was before?"

Gerry: "Well, there was a big and immediate personality change. Where his conversation had been wide ranging over many topics, now it was restricted solely to aspects of his firing and his plans for reinstatement.———"(p127)

Gerry went on to describe the deterioration in Blaine's appearance and the partial paralysis and speech problems resulting from his heart attack and strokes. When Sheridan tried to discredit his testimony because he was not a doctor and accused him of only inferring or speculating as to the cause of Blaine's health problems, Gerry responded:

"But a speculation based on the fact that here is a pattern of known behavior. There comes his termination and a personality change is immediately effected. I tend to make a connection on that." (p133)

As his wife and caregiver, there was never any doubt in my mind that Blaine's health was severely effected by the gross treatment he received at the lottery and the stress related to his battle for vindication. Friends such as Gerry and family members all observed this. I think my testimony and that of Gerry's was important to counteract the erroneous impression that Sheridan tried to convey to the jury that Blaine was arrogant and insisted on having his own way. That description applied to the three defendants, Mazzola and Sheridan himself, —not Blaine. In any case, Blaine's lawsuit was not for the harm to his health. It was for wrongful termination and the deprivation of his freedom of speech.

J. Blaine Lewis, Jr.

(pp32-196)

Blaine was on the witness stand all day on December 4, 1996, and if Sheridan and Vacchelli from the Attorney General's office thought they could take advantage of him due to his strokes, especially his speech stroke, they were mistaken. Having been so articulate before his speech stroke made it very frustrating for him, but he had worked hard to regain his speech, and he accomplished his goal of speaking well enough to testify in court. He wanted his day in court and he wanted the justice he deserved. He received that justice from the jury, but that justice was stolen by the Appellate court.

I was so proud of Blaine as he answered the questions clearly and completely concerning his background, the makeup of the Division of Special Revenue, his responsibilities as unit head of the lottery, and the statutes and regulations which provided strict controls for state-sponsored gambling with regard to the Gaming Policy Board and appointments of unit heads as well as the executive director. He explained many of the ways he concerned himself with security and good public relations. He explained his staff meetings and his team approach to running the lottery. He explained his efforts to gain more knowledge of lotteries by studying those in other countries and other states, his presidency of the North American Association of State and Provincial Lotteries (NASPL) and the educational purpose of the organization. He recalled articles he had written for Public Gaming International, an international magazine dealing with lotteries.

He told about his recommending a lotto game and how his boss put it on hold for a year. He explained his desire to join a new multi-state lotto called Lotto America in the '80's but was told to forget about it. Lotto America became Powerball, and Connecticut finally joined it in 1995.

Question: "Did you have any prior—prior to this incident in your termination in—, had you obeyed orders?"

Blaine: "Yes, even ones I didn't enjoy. I obeyed them, but I was never ordered to lie." (p52)

Question: "Did the typically short tenure time in office of executive directors and Gaming Policy Board members affect you in any way?"

Blaine: "Yes. I was concerned about it. I thought some day they'd get us in trouble and they did. Actually, I'm sure they were experienced in business, but had very little experience in lotteries." (p52)

Question: "Did the experience you were having with the executive director and the Gaming Policy Board members on occasion—how did that make you feel about your duties and your —"

Blaine: "I needed to be far more conscientious, more responsible to watch over things." (p52)

Blaine then told of the length of time each of the defendants had been with the Division and their lack of experience with regard to gaming operations.

Question: "What were the events in January 1988 and in May of 1988 that caused you concern about the decisions being made by, among other people, these defendants?"

Blaine: "Because in spite of the fact that they were warned by me and other people, they awarded the contract to General Instrument for the on-line system. That was in January. And in May, in spite of the fact that I warned against it and other people warned against it, they permitted General Instrument to go on-line with their system and cause big problems." (pp55-56)

Blaine then answered questions about the on-line system, his research into General Instruments's past performance in other states, and his efforts to express his reservations to the executive director and the Gaming Policy Board. He then gave details about the testing which showed that GI was not ready to go on-line in May 1988. A memo from Faraci in the Department of Administrative Services for the state of Connecticut and a memo from Acayan, the unit head of the Licensing and Integrity Assurance unit of the Division were introduced as exhibits. Both these memos were strongly supportive of Blaine's views. Blaine identified some of his warning memos and they too were introduced as exhibits. After answering questions about the disaster when GI went on-line:

Question: "Was GI subject to fines as a result?"

Blaine: "Yes, according to the contract." (p86)

Question: "And how much was that fine?"

Blaine: "Well, we couldn't find out because it wasn't possible to fine (sic) it because General Instrument didn't provide the information necessary for us to calculate the fine. So we had to set up a team of accountants, five of them including two CPAs, to study it to try to decide and guess, really, what the fine was." (p86)

Question: "And was the fine a subject of negotiation?"

Blaine: "It was not supposed to be. The contract didn't call for it, but the Division did special interest for special assistance for GI to ——permit them to negotiate the fine."

Question: "How much was the negotiated fine?"

Blaine: "Negotiated down to 1.76 million dollars." (p87)

Question: "And what was your estimate of what the fine should have been?"

Blaine: "Over $2,000,000, about 2.2 million."

Question: "Now, Mr. Lewis, I'm showing you four exhibits here; N, O, P, Q—actually five. Would you take them in order and describe—just identify what they are?"

Blaine: "This is a letter to GI from Mr. Ragazzi officially notifying them that they were not living up to the contract."

Question: "And what is that one?"

Blaine: "Instructions from Mr. Drakeley, Mr. Hickey's deputy, changing the way the assignments—the fine should be adjusted—should be awarded, should be done."

Question: "And what is that?"

Blaine: "That's a memo to Ragazzi from Eric Meder, who was assistant unit head of LIA, who was Mr. Acayan's deputy. He had had some problems experienced with GIC on accounting problems and within the LIA, what problems it was causing the accountants." (pp87-88)

Question: "And what is that one?"

Blaine: "That was from Richard Fradette, who's chief financial examiner for the Division."

Question: "Did they have to do with attempting to calculate the losses?"

Blaine: "Yes. He was one of the CPAs on it."

Question: "And what about this one?"

Blaine: "It was a memo to Mr. Drakeley from Mr. Ragazzi about the notices of noncompliance to GI."

Question: "In other words, this was to do with notifying GI of their breach?"

Blaine: "Right"

Question: "And with respect to the breakdown?"

Blaine: "Right" (p88)

All 5 memos dealing with the violations of the contract and the fines were submitted as exhibits N, O, P, Q and R.

Exhibit S was a Mailgram sent to the executive director with copies to Governor O'Neill, Blaine and Barbara Porto. It was typical of the frustration and hundreds of calls concerning the breakkdown after GI went on-line. It was sent from J. O'Toole:

"Dear Sir, I am sending this letter now because, as a citizen of Connecticut and a lottery agent, I believe we have a problem. This lottery system is not working right. I have held off writing until this new system was up for a while.

"First, when we call with a problem, we are put on hold. Then we are told to shut off the machine. (That, by the way, is their stock answer.) We were never told why the problem is there.

———

"When we are trying to cash winning tickets, the machine states 'wrong Julian year'. When asked why this happens, we're told to call the state liaison people would inform us. When calling the state people, they have no idea what GI was talking about. GI's answer is shut off the machine. This is 6:00 p.m. with people in line to play the numbers.——

"We also understand that the GI people ignore the state liaison people. We know they ignore us. I understand you get paid whether you sell one ticket or a million tickets. We don't.

"I'm beginning to wonder if this new system was political and not financial for the state. As an agent, I think this should be investigated. As a citizen, I know it should be. Sincerely" (pp90-91)

Blaine went on to answer questions about the gag order, why it was really aimed at him, since it was the lottery that was in the newspapers every day. He explained the importance of public trust and the hiring of a new state employee, a public information officer to respond to the press. With reference to the gag order:

Question: "To your knowledge, did Mr. Cowen and Mr. Hickey and Mr. Lange, were they aware of this order?"

Blaine: "They had to be because it was in the newspaper."

Question: "Did they ever express any concern about it?"

Blaine: "No." (p95)

Question: "Was it your understanding that they approved the order?"

Blaine: "Yes, because it's their job to oversee the Division." (p95)

Question: "now, did Mr. Hickey ever say anything to you that revealed his true feelings—"

Blaine: "Yes."

Question: "What did he say?"

Blaine: "During our meetings in May when I was being – getting ready to terminate me, He told me when he was telling me not to speak in public about the game, he told me that he wouldn't put up with what happened in 1988."

Question: "Did he further describe what he considered that to be?"

Blaine: "It was an abuse to the Division and to the Board."

(p96)

Blaine then answered questions concerning GI's pushing a change in the lotto game:

Question: "What did you feel that the change that they were proposing would do to sales and net revenues to the state?"

Blaine: "Exactly what it did, bring them down."

Question: "Did you—was this idea of the vendor proposing such a change, was this something new?"

Blaine: "Yes, very new. We never did it before. The lottery always designed its own games." (p101)

Blaine explained that he wrote memos to the Board answering dozens of questions they had as they looked into it. He provided them with analysis and studies to show why it should not be done. He established by minutes of the Board meetings that the three defendants were all aware of his opposition to the game change and the reasons for that opposition.

Question: "And what happened in February and March and April –well, the first four months of '89, what happened to lottery sales and why?"

Blaine: "Well, the terminals were just getting finished. They were finally finished in April and the first four months of '89, Lotto sales were 27.4 percent higher than they were in the preceding year, which shows the problem was not with the game. The problem was with the system, as we changed the system and not the game at that point. Also, we had several sales records during that time."

Question: "What – were there other changes in the lottery unit in the works at that time also?"

Blaine: "Yes. We were designing a change in the instant game so we would deliver and have more than one game on the street at a time, but we couldn't do it with our existing bank system that we had. We couldn't do it. So we were designing a system so we could get more than one game on the street, which would increase instant sales." (p107)

Question: "Was there also another drop-off system, so-called? Will you explain that?"

Blaine: "Yes. Instead of having the banks have the tickets,

forcing the agents to go to the banks, we were going to set up a system which required hiring people and also buying vans. So we could personally deliver the tickets to the agents instead of dropping them off at banks and forcing agents to go to the banks and pick them up, which is the way it had always been in the past from the beginning of the lottery."

Question: "And so what would be the effect of that?"

Blaine: "Hopefully, that would help instant sales."

Question: "—the purpose of that was to increase revenues?"

Blaine: "To the state, yes." (p108)

Blaine explained how he only much later found out about the meeting before May 15 between Hickey, Cowen and Lange. He described the meetings starting on May 15, 1989 when Hickey ordered him to present the change in Lotto to the Board in a positive manner.

Question: "When Mr. Hickey ordered you verbally on May 15th and on May 16th to present this change to Cowen and Lange in a positive manner, what did that mean?"

Blaine: "Positive; all positives and no negatives. All pros and no cons."

Question: "And did he expect you in that way to endorse the change?"

Blaine: "Yes" (p121)

Question: "So what did you feel that the purpose of the order was?"

Blaine: "To cover up their previous mistakes."

Question: "I mean to you personally?"

Blaine: "To silence me." (p122)

Question: "What else did he say when he gave you that order not to speak publicly about his order that he had just given you? Did he make any remarks about what happened a year earlier when the system broke down?"

Blaine: "Yes. He said that when I spoke about it in public, he would not put up with it like that again and it was an abuse to the Board and to the Division."

Question: "And so that's why he ordered you on May 18th to be quiet?"

Blaine: "Right."

Question: "What else did he do? What did you say to him when he said that?"

Blaine: "I told him he was putting me in a box and then my thoughts were that in the past, the Division had made two big mistakes and each time I warned them against them and each time I was silenced because of it and take my freedom of speech away.

First time was in January of '88 when I warned them about not awarding the contract to General Instrument and they awarded it and I was ordered not to speak publicly about it. Mr. Ragazzi told me not to speak publicly about the awarding of the contract.

And the second time was in May when I warned them and/ or people warned them not to permit General Instrument to go on-line with the system and they permitted it and then I was— we had a big mess with the system and I was gagged.

Then I was thinking, now, the third time they are ordering me to not speak publicly about it and in addition, they are or- dering me to lie about it. I told them I can't do it."

Question: "Take your time. And so what did Mr. Hickey do?"

Blaine: "He put me on leave."

Next came answers concerning the Loudermill hearing that took place on May 24. Blaine was informed of the hearing on May 22. His request for additional time to prepare and find an attorney was denied. He found an attorney and his attorney's formal request for additional time to become familiar with the case and prepare was also denied.

The addition of Blaine's personnel matter was added to the agenda of the May 25th Board meeting just prior to the meeting, and Blaine's counsel was not advised of this until the meeting started. In describing the May 26th meeting:

Blaine: "Well, ———Mr. Hickey was given 15 minutes, and he was never interrupted, to speak about why I should be fired. Then they gave me time and I started and then they re- peatedly interrupted me so it was difficult for me to put my record, my message, my thoughts on the record. They interrupted me repeatedly and I managed to get in the part that I was going to put in about saying I was willing to present the game in a balanced way to the Board."

Question: "Did they acknowledge that in any way?"

Blaine: "No; pretended they didn't hear it." (p146)

When Sheridan cross-examined Blaine, with regard to Cowen, Lange and Hickey, all Board members at the time, not directly ordering Blaine to remain silent after GI went on-line in May 1988:

Question: "Who did?"

Blaine: "Mr. Ragazzi and he gave the gag order to me and it was in the newspaper and they certainly knew about it and they didn't do anything about it. It was their job to do something about it."

Question: "Do you know if Ragazzi asked them for permission to issue this order to you?"

Blaine: "No but he certainly did not agree with the Constitution. He certainly should have asked their opinion or permission, if you will, because he was violating the Constitution, which he later admitted because he took the order away saying that I could have free speech."

Question: "So as far as you're concerned, one of their duties is to insure that nobody's constitutional rights are violated?

Blaine: "That's correct."

Question: "Is that in the statute somewhere? Did I miss that? Is that part of their duties?"

Blaine: "To supervise the operation or oversee the operation of the system. Obeying the law should be part of it."

Question: "But they only meet once a month; correct?"

Blaine: "That's right, but they have telephones." (169-170)

Sheridan continued to be combative, and Blaine continued to stand up to him.

Blaine remained concerned about how much his speech problems might have interfered with his testimony. I kept reassuring him that he had done extremely well. I will always be grateful that we received a copy of the trial transcript just a few days before his fatal fall on October 9, 2000. He read his testimony and with a twinkle in his eye he said he hadn't done too badly after all. No, Blaine was terrific, and it was not his fault that his justice was stolen by the Appellate court based on what we both knew were lies and fabrications from the Attorney General's office.

THE STALLING GAME

I was regaining my strength after my chemotherapy, surgery and radiation treatment for breast cancer in 1999. I had not regained any of the 20 pounds lost and still could not sleep without sleeping pills. I was grateful however that I had been able to care for Blaine throughout the whole ordeal and to give him the support he needed when we learned in October 1999 that the U. S. Supreme Court had denied his petition. It was devastating to learn that lawyers in the state Attorney General's office could lie and get away with it. It was even more difficult to accept the injustice from the Courts. We had both felt that in the United States, if you had the law on your side, and you had the strength to persist, you would eventually receive justice. It took us more than 10 years to discover how wrong we were.

Our earlier attempts to gain permission to sue the state had been denied. One cannot sue the state without its permission, and the State Legislature's Judiciary Committee had denied that permission. The injustice had been so gross and the actions against Blaine so vindictive that our State Representative, Sonya (Sonny) Googins felt that the State Legislature should at least pass a bill to compensate Blaine for what the state actually owed him since 1989. She would have to introduce such a bill before the end of February in order to have time for the Legislature to act. At this time, January 2000, the state had never paid Blaine the vacation pay and sick pay owed since May 1989 or the pension and health benefits he never received from June 1989 to March 1993.

Blaine requested these payments in February 1993, from Alan Mazzola, who at that time was personnel director of the Division of Special Revenue. Blaine's lawyers made a formal request in writing in October 1995. If the interest was calculated starting in March 1993, when he requested payment, the state owed Blaine $215,020 as of March 1, 2000. If the interest was

107

calculated starting in October 1995, when the formal request was made in writing, the state owed Blaine $182,387 as of March 1, 2000.

Because the lawyers in the Attorney General's office had lied on their appeal and briefs to the 2nd Circuit Court of Appeals and again in their briefs to the U.S. Supreme Court, Blaine and I had lost all confidence in their integrity. The case had dragged on for 10 years. Bill Rogers, Blaine's attorney for most of those years, had retired. Other attorneys in the same firm had taken over Blaine's case. The state's attorneys convinced them in phone conversations that the state would compensate Blaine fairly and that they should meet to iron out the details. They cleverly stalled and stalled and finally agreed to the meeting on February 28. When that meeting finally took place, Blaine's attorneys were stunned. Assistant Attorney General Robert F. Vacchelli and Alan Mazzola were willing to pay Blaine his vacation pay that they admitted they owed him, but without any interest only if Blaine would sign a release or waiver for the sick pay and almost 4 years with no pension. They had successfully stalled to the point where it was too late for our State Representative to introduce a bill in that session of the legislature. Blaine refused to sign the waiver. It was difficult to believe that the Attorney General, Richard Blumenthal was not aware of what Vacchelli and Mazzola were doing. It was difficult to believe that they could behave so despicably. They had successfully conned our attorneys. Sonny Googins told us it was now too late to do anything in this session but she would submit a bill to the Judiciary Committee to take care of the injustice in the next 2001 session of the Legislature.

Several months later, in July 2000, despite the fact that Blaine had refused to sign a waiver, he received a check to compensate him for the vacation pay owed him. He was in Yale-New Haven Hospital at the time. There was no interest added and it was only a small portion of what was owed him.

If Blaine had received the justice he deserved, he would have received just over $2 million ($2,048,853.20) in December 1996. This would have included attorney's fees. The economist, Dr. Richard Martin, in his testimony under oath at the Federal District trial on December 5, 1996 calculated Blaine's losses at $514,098. That would have been what was owed him as of the trial date and assumed Blaine would have retired in February 1992, had he not been fired. The jury awarded Blaine $1,028,196 in compensatory damages for the violation of his First Amendment Right to Free Speech and his State Law claim of wrongful termination. They awarded him $640,644 in punitive damages for the violation of his First Amendment Right to Free Speech.

Blaine had not signed a waiver, and he still expected Sonny Googins to introduce bills in future sessions of the legislature to pay him what was still owed him—no attorney's fees, no damages for being fired for refusing to lie, no punitive damages,—just what the state owed him. If March 1993 was used as the starting date for adding interest, the state would owe Blaine $200,408 as of March 2001.

The year 2000 had started badly. It was ironic that our tax dollars were helping to pay the salaries of the very people that were abusing their power and inflicting such injustice. Blaine had been a model state manager, intelligent, industrious, and always putting the good of Connecticut's citizens first. One can only wonder why his political bosses proved to be so incompetent and why they had behaved so reprehensibly.

It was a terrible injustice and it was still early in the year 2000.

SUMMARY OF CRUCIAL ERRORS IN APPEAL TO THE 2ND CIRCUIT

These errors were the basis for the erroneous Reversal by the 2nd Circuit

Richard Blumenthal, Attorney General
Robert F. Vacchelli, Assistant Attorney General
Contrary to papers filed with the court, Aaron S. Bayer, Deputy Attorney General, presented the state's case, not Robert F. Vacchelli.

1. "Lewis was a High-Ranking Policymaker."

(This error was fabricated for the first time in appeal and never claimed at trial.) Hickey, Cowen and Lange had been appointed by the Governor. They were the policymakers. Lewis was a manager and could not choose lottery vendors, postpone a new vendor from going on-line when he knew they were not ready, hire personnel, add or change lottery games on his own, have Connecticut join a multi-state lotto game, or even speak for the lottery after the May 1988 gag order. This was a convenient fabrication to support the erroneous contention that the defendants were due Qualified Immunity.

With that aside the defendants then went on to claim that Lewis *improperly arrogated* to himself the authority to set agency policy. He did not. He merely wanted to present his views for the Board to consider. That, however, was an admission by the defendants that Lewis was not a policymaker. He did not have the authority to set agency policy.

2 "He stated that he planned to rebuke the project publicly at the very meeting where he was being asked to introduce it, calling that a 'balanced' presentation."

111

(This error was also fabricated for the first time in appeal and is completely opposite to the trial record.) The record shows that at both the Pre-Termination hearing of May 24, 1989 and again at the Board meeting of May 26, 1989 he clearly stated that he was willing to give the pros and cons of changing the Lotto game. He obviously knew the definition of "balanced".

3. "Lewis' position would bring all Board business to a halt." There should have been no new actions by the Board, which is what the Legislature intended when it wisely required by Statute a quorum of 4 to take action. The clear and erroneous implication is that the Division's business would have come to a halt.

4. "Lewis was ordered to present the 'Division's Views'." Exhibits and testimony at trial by both Lewis and Drakeley prove that not only was this term not used, but it was Lewis' views that were to be represented, not the Division's View's. He was not a parrot. His value to the Division was his analysis based on his knowledge and experience.

ERRORS IN DEFENDANTS' BRIEF-2nd CIRCUIT

Richard Blumenthal, Attorney General and
Robert F. Vacchelli, Assistant Attorney General

P 4 (bottom) "All other Unit Heads and the lottery contractor agreed with the change."

All other Unit Heads did not agree with the change. Hickey stated that they did but there was no evidence submitted to support this. The idea to change the odds for Lotto originated with the lottery contractor.

P 5 (line 7) "Lewis refused in writing."

5/17/89 memo requested Hickey to withdraw order with good reason.

On 5/18/89 he refused orally to present the game change to the GPB in a positive manner. He had been ordered to lie.

P 5 (lines 15-17) "He clung to this belief despite a previously issued opinion of the Attorney General stating that the Board could act notwithstanding the vacancies."

He did not hear of the acting Attorney General's opinion until 5/24/89 at the Loudermill hearing.

P 5 (bottom) "He stated that he planned to rebuke the project publicly at the very meeting where he was being asked to introduce it, calling that a "balanced" presentation."

The evidence clearly shows that he called a "balanced" presentation one that presented the pros and cons. There was no evidence presented that he planned to rebuke the project publicly because there was none.

P 6 (lines 2-4) "Lewis' position on the composition of the Board not only contradicted a controlling Attorney General opin-

113

ion, but if followed would bring all Board business a halt."

He had not heard of the Acting Attorney General's opinion. The opinion, he found out later, was for a Board of 3 members with a footnote extending it to 2 members. With the Board being minimal in size, the opinion being just that, an opinion, an increase in the Board to achieve a quorum of 4 would without question make any actions by the Board legal. Failure of the Board to take new action would not have brought the Division's business to a halt.

P 6 (footnote) "In fact, after the public controversy that followed the Lewis' termination, the Lotto did slip in popularity, even though lottery games in general increased in popularity during the same period."

The public controversy was substantially created by firing him. He was correct in judging how the public would react to making the Lotto game almost twice as difficult to win. The controversy over his firing did not stop instant games from an increase in sales, thanks largely to Lewis' preparations for changes that were carried out.

P 7 (line 6 of Summary of Argument) "The decision was Hickey's to make and Lewis' to carry out by presenting it to the Gaming Policy Board for approval."

The decision was for Hickey *and* the Board to make. Hickey could have presented it to the Board himself. In fact, he had Ziemak recommend it to the Board, with no negatives, on 5/25/89.

P 9 (2nd par. Lines 7-10) "For example, the plaintiff claimed that he refused to present the policy change to the Board because, with three vacant positions, the Board was not legally constituted and authorized to act."

The plaintiff never discussed the legality of the Board in the trial.

P 11 (lines 3-7) "Should a plaintiff demonstrate these factors, the defendant has the opportunity to demonstrate by a pre-ponderance of the evidence that it should have undertaken the same adverse employment action ' even in the absence of the protected conduct.'"

The defendants never claimed or threatened to fire the plaintiff for any reason other than for disobeying the order to lie.

P 11 (line 10-11) "...for what he would not say."

He would have given the pros if he had been permitted to give the cons.

P 11 (Par. A) "To be protected, the speech must be on a matter of public concern, and the employee's interest in express-ing (him)self on this matter must not be outweighed by any in-jury the speech could cause to 'the interest of the state, as an employer, in promoting the efficiency of the public services it performs through its employees.'"

The speech in this case would have been beneficial to the state, not an injury. From 1988 to 1995 revenues to the state from lotto dropped by 193 million dollars ($193,000,000). The Board might have been hesitant to change the game had Lewis been allowed to give his analysis, pros and cons, at the public meeting.

P 16 (lines 5-8) "He believed he could not criticize the plan publicly, as he had in the past criticized other Board actions....once he had presented the plan favorably."

His motivation was to present his views publicly in the hopes of saving the public from a change which he felt would, and in fact did, cripple the Lotto game and cut state revenues. In response to a direct question, in May 1988, several days after the General Instrument on-line system crashed, he responded truthfully that he had not favored the change in vendors. After that he was gagged and not allowed to speak publicly on Lottery matters. He had always been most respectful of the Board as minutes of Board meetings will readily show.

P 17 (last 3 lines) "(3) the employer took action against the employee based on this disruption and not in retaliation for the speech."

There was no disruption until the plaintiff was fired and the Lotto game changed. His remaining silent could not have caused a disruption.

P 19 (lines 11-12) ".....to present the change in a positive way, which the plaintiff construed to mean in a favorable way (only pros, no cons)."

Construed indicates the plaintiff was incorrect. Drakeley was a witness and testified at trial that the plaintiff's understanding was correct.

P 19 (line 17) "....representing the Division's views."

The "Division's views" was invented after the plaintiff was fired, and after the December 1996 trial. It was clear to the plaintiff that he was being asked to misrepresent his own views. This was also what Drakeley understood and testified to at trial.

P 20 (lines 3-4) "The plaintiff, however, wished to present his own views to the Board, not the agency's views."

Views did not become agency views until the Board took action. Even though he was not a policymaker, he was part of the agency and his value to the state was his ability to express his views concerning his field of expertise. In this case he was willing to express Hickey's and General Instrument's views as well.

P 20 (last par.) "In short, the plaintiff improperly arrogated to himself the authority to set agency policy,......."

The defendants have argued throughout that the plaintiff was a Policymaker. This was one of the principal errors on which the 2nd Circuit based its reversal. Here the defendants falsely accuse the plaintiff of improperly arrogating to himself the authority to be a policymaker, thus claiming he was not a Policymaker. Which was it? He was clearly not a Policymaker and he was merely desirous of giving all views or remaining silent as an alternative to lying.

P 20 (lines 5-6 from bottom) "......a policy question that was ultimately Hickey's responsibility to resolve for the agency."

It was Hickey's and the Board's responsibility, not Hickey's. Here Lewis is no longer a policymaker, but 9 lines before this he is again referred to as a "policy-making employee".

P 21 (note 8) " There is in this case absolutely no hint that the defendants had engaged in criminal or unethical conduct that the plaintiff was seeking to reveal."

In depositions as well as at trial, the defendants admitted to a secret meeting, not known to the plaintiff, where they had agreed on a Lotto change. The meeting was clearly illegal and shows that they were ready to vote on the change independent of what the plaintiff would say. It was therefore a pretext to ask the plaintiff to lie, knowing that he was a man of integrity and would not lie. His refusal to lie would be the excuse for firing him. The defendants engaged in both illegal and unethical behavior.

P 22 (line 1) ".....in reality he was putting the Division in a box."

They were never in a box. They voted for the change after Ziemak's positive presentation the day before the plaintiff was fired. They could have voted for it even if the plaintiff had given the balanced presentation that he was not allowed to give.

P 22 (lines 3-6) "By calling this his right to free speech, he thereby sought to immunize himself from any termination, while at the same time holding the approved plan hostage to his own opposition."

He was not thinking of termination and certainly had no idea that the defendants were setting him up to be terminated. He was trying to do what was right for the citizens of the state and this caused his termination. The plan was not approved until the Board voted for it and it was in no way being held hostage.

P 23 (lines 15-17) "Thus, the disruption to the governmental program was clearly predictable even by the plaintiff; in fact it was his acknowledged aim."

There was no discussion or evidence anywhere to indicate that anyone thought that leaving the Lotto game alone would be disruptive. Quite to the contrary, changing the game proved to be disastrous. The plaintiff's acknowledged aim was to protect state revenues. He could not create a disruption by not speaking. He preferred to remain silent rather than lie. This is simply another fabrication, without evidence, because there is none.

P 30 (line 12) ".....a policy-making, at-will employee...."

In order to argue for Qualified Immunity for the defendants the plaintiff here is called a "policy-making" employee. The defendants see-saw repeatedly as to the plaintiff being a "Policymaker" and one who did not follow the order to lie given by his supervisor, who was the "Policymaker". He could not be both at the same time. He, in fact was not a policymaker.

P 35 (lines 1-3) "The plaintiff spent a considerable amount of time testifying and arguing to the jury that the Board was not 'duly constituted' because it did not have the full complement of five members."

The trial transcript will show that the plaintiff spent *zero* time discussing the above. This was not discussed since the charges of violations of state law, Statutes and Division regulations were dropped. They were never adjudicated. This fabrication was invented so that the defendants could unjustifiably complain that the Attorney General's Opinion was not allowed as evidence. It was not relevant to the trial.

P 41 (footnote) "....he should not have made his bald statements maligning the Board's composition."

It is the defendants making bald statements maligning the plaintiff by insisting that he testified about the composition of the Board when he in fact did not. The defendants go on for pages on the matter of the irrelevant opinion when in fact they should be embarrassed by it.

P 43 (lines 3-5) "Thus, as the Magistrate Judge admitted post-trial, the jury based its $514,098 award for humiliation and emotional distress only on plaintiff's and his wife's testimony."

The defendants surely know that the plaintiff's physical appearance and speech problems were obvious to the jury. Not only was there testimony concerning his humiliation and distress by his wife, who was his caregiver, but also there was testimony on this matter by two others, a social friend and a former Lottery employee.

P 44 (lines 12-13) "...who refused to follow orders to run his unit...."

The plaintiff never refused to run his unit. The unit was operating very successfully. The plaintiff refused to misrepresent himself, that is to lie, in a public Board meeting.

P 47 (lines 5-8) "As his expert economist testified, however, it would have been to his financial benefit for him to retire immediately in 1989 and begin receiving the pension."

The defendants know full well that the plaintiff could not request his pension without the defendants then calling that a waiver of his right to sue to be reinstated. He could not request his pension until his Administrative appeal had been decided. That was in February 1993. The expert's comments were taken out of context. Obviously the plaintiff would have had more financial benefit had he collected the pension for those four years rather than not collect it.

P 48 (lines 3-4 from bottom) "....Years after the termination plaintiff's doctor still found him fit."

The doctor found him fit 2 years after he was fired. This case and the subsequent stress went on for years. He did not have his heart attack and first of several strokes for 3 years. That was after Judge Norko reversed Judge Freed's earlier decision that he had a "contested case" and a right to an administrative appeal.

REVERSAL BY THE UNITED STATES COURT OF APPEALS FOR THE SECOND CIRCUIT

Decided Jan. 15, 1999, Docket No. 97-7895

Before: Kearse and Walker, Circuit Judges, and Weinstein, District Judge

Quotes from Decision written by Walker:

P 5 (lines 10-12) "Part of his job was to communicate with the media and the public as, in his own words, 'the official lottery spokesman.'"

Lewis was gagged in May 1988 and was forbidden from speaking to the press. In January 1989, the order was modified to restore his free speech as long as he made it clear that he was not speaking for the lottery. Both the original order and the modification were entered as exhibits in the Federal District trial in December 1996.

P 6 (lines 14-15) "The directive was eventually withdrawn, although the Division's public information officer remained."

The directive was modified January 4, 1989 to read that he must make it clear that he was not speaking for the lottery: "The employee must state clearly however, that in expressing opinions or making statements the employee is not acting as a spokesman for the Division or purporting to express its views or policies."

P 8 (lines 6-7) "The reduced Board consisted of Hickey and defendants Cowen and Lange."

The reduced Board consisted of 2 members, Cowen and

Lange. Hickey was the Executive Director.

P 8 (lines 8-11) "Hickey testified that prior to May 18, he simply asked Lewis to keep the matter confidential until Lewis made his decision as to whether he would follow Hickey's order. According to Hickey, Lewis refused to remain silent and Hickey let the matter drop."

Hickey lied under oath. Lewis did remain silent as ordered and the defendants submitted no evidence to the contrary.

P 8 (lines 13-23)

There is no mention of the fact that Drakeley was at the May 18 meeting and that Drakeley testified at the trial and corroborated Lewis' description of the order.

P 9 (line 9) "….because Lewis failed to attend the meeting…."

Lewis had been put on leave and his council was not notified of the meeting until it had already started.

P 15 (lines 6-24) "…..The government bears the burden of demonstrating that the speech threatens to interfere with government operations…………"

Lewis did not speak. It was not possible for his non-speech to threaten to interfere with government operations.

P 16 This whole page deals with the Pickering balance test which is about balancing the damage to the state with the violation of free speech.(lines 6-9) "The more the employee's speech touches on matters of significant public concern, the greater the level of disruption to the government that must be shown."

The jury concluded that the violation of free speech outweighed the alleged threat of disruption. To tilt the balance in favor of the defendants, the 2nd Circuit had to decide erroneously, that Lewis had been ordered to represent the "Division's views" instead of his own personal views and that his silence would cause a disruption.

P 19 (lines 1-5) "However, even if the Pickering balance is resolved in the employer's favor, the employee may still demonstrate liability by proving that the employer disciplined the employee in retaliation for the speech, rather than out of fear of the disruption."

There could have been no fear of disruption since there was no speech. However, Lewis did show that this was retaliation for speech 1 year earlier when the defendants went against Lewis' advice as to vendor and then the vendor's readiness to go on-line.

Their decisions were disastrous to the state and Lewis was gagged. Their lack of action indicates they approved of the gagging and that they were resentful.

P 19 (lines 21-23) "Lewis has not presented evidence that the defendants acted out of an improper desire to retaliate against Lewis, ..."

It would be next to impossible for Lewis to prove an improper desire to retaliate. The evidence certainly points to it.

P 22 (lines 10-13) ".....Both Hickey and Drakeley testified that Lewis' refusal to promote the proposed change would result in negative publicity and decreased morale,...."

Lewis refused to *propose* the change. He clearly stated, on the record, many times that he would implement the change if accepted. This would not have been the first time that he promoted Lottery decisions with which he disagreed.

P 23 (lines 2-4) "In sum, Hickey and Drakeley testified that Lewis' refusal to promote the change undermined the Lottery Unit's ability to do its job."

Hickey and Drakeley were answering questions about the effects of bad publicity and the effects of his not promoting the game. Lewis made it clear that he would promote the game, if accepted.

P 23 (lines 16-18) " Finally, Lewis' refusal meant that the office would be deprived of its principal spokesperson on a matter of public policy at a public meeting before the Board."

Lewis was not the spokesperson for the Lottery. One year earlier, the Division appointed an official spokesperson for all the Units including the Lottery Unit. The Board would not have been deprived of Lewis' analysis if he had been able to represent his views and analysis. Certainly, that was his function and one that promoted sound public policy.

P 24 (lines 3-5) "Lewis was a senior policymaking employee, whose job required confidentiality and public contact."

Lewis was not a policymaking employee, whose job required confidentiality and public contact. It not only did not require public contact, it discouraged public contact. He ceased being a Lottery spokesman one year earlier.

P 24 (lines 21-24) "Moreover, we cannot second-guess the judgement of Lewis' supervisors that effective operation of the lottery was dependent upon the proposed change being implemented."

The 2nd Circuit did not have to second-guess the judgement of Lewis' supervisors. One of the plaintiff's exhibits had a chart showing that from 1988 to 1995, revenues to the state from lotto dropped 193 million dollars ($193,000,000). The proposed change proved disastrous.

P 25 (lines 16-20) "The defendants did not violate Lewis' First Amendment rights by terminating him based on Hickey's reasonable belief that Lewis' refusal to present the change to the Board in a 'positive' manner might impair Division operations."

Hickey had been on the job for approximately 2 weeks. Lewis had been with the lottery for 16 years. A more reasonable reaction would be to make the change despite Lewis' analysis. It was not reasonable to expect Lewis to lie. It turns out that Lewis' belief that the change itself would harm the lotto game was reasonable. Hickey's supposed "reasonable belief" was obviously an excuse for firing Lewis.

P 27 (lines 15-19) "Lewis was directed to present the Division's views, not his own. Although Lewis understood Hickey's order to mean that he should "lie" to the Board, there is no evidence that Hickey or anyone else ordered Lewis to misrepresent either the facts or his personal views to the Board."

When Hickey gave his order to Lewis, the term, "Division's Views", was never used. They could not be the Division's views until the Board took action. There were no exhibits submitted that indicate he would be only presenting the Division's views. There is ample evidence in the trial, testimony from both Lewis and Drakeley that Hickey did order Lewis to misrepresent the facts and his personal views to the Board.

REVERSAL ISSUES IN DECISION BY 2nd CIRCUIT

POLICYMAKER ISSUE

Blaine was only able to make recommendations to the Executive Director and the Gaming Policy Board. They were appointed by the Governor. They were the Policymakers. For example:

Blaine could not select the advertising agency. That was done by a committee with limited representation of the Lottery Unit.

Blaine wanted Connecticut to join Lotto America, a multistate lottery. The Executive Director said no. Lotto America became Powerball and Connecticut joined that after Blaine was fired.

Blaine could not choose the Lottery vendors. He was against giving the on-line contract to General Instrument in 1988, but his opinion was ignored.

When Blaine warned that General Instrument was not prepared to go on-line in May 1988, his opinion was again ignored. The system immediately crashed and the rebuilding of all the terminals was not completed until April 1989.

Blaine could not add or change Lottery games without the Gaming Policy Board's approval.

Blaine could not authorize his trip to his last meeting of NASPL, the North American Association of State and Provincial Lotteries, even though he was then president of the organization. He had to go on his own time with no reimbursement for travel expenses.

Blaine could not have anything to do with public relations

after he was gagged in May 1988. When he finally was given permission to speak publicly in January 1989, he had to make it clear that he was not representing the Lottery, but speaking for himself.

Blaine could not hire people to work in the Lottery.

The term, Policymaker, was never used in the trial in the Federal District Court in December 1996. Senior lawyers in the Attorney General's office used it for the first time in the appeal to the 2nd Circuit Court of Appeals. This was one of the errors on which the reversal was based.

DIVISION POLICY

When Blaine was given the order to lie to the Gaming Policy Board in May 1989, he was being asked to misrepresent himself. The Executive Director, who gave him the order said nothing about "Division policy". It could not be "Division policy" until the Gaming Policy Board voted for it. Blaine offered to give his analysis of the game change to the Gaming Policy Board, both pros and cons. It would then be up to a legal Board to determine what was "Division policy". His offer to give his analysis to the Board was rejected. Despite the testimony by Blaine and testimony by William Drakeley, the assistant to the Executive Director, who was present when the order to lie was given, senior lawyers in the Attorney General's office claimed that the order was "Division policy" in the appeal to the 2nd Circuit Court of Appeals. This was another error on which the reversal was based.

QUALIFIED IMMUNITY

The right of freedom of speech is a clearly established right under the Constitution of the state of Connecticut as well as the United States Constitution of which a reasonable person should have known. Senior lawyers in the Attorney General's office argued for Qualified Immunity in the appeal to the 2nd Circuit Court of Appeals based on the fictitious "Division View". This was still another error on which the reversal was based.

THREATS TO OBSTRUCT PROCESS

In the appeal to the 2nd Circuit the Attorney General's lawyers stated "He stated that he planned to rebuke the project publicly at the very next meeting where he was being asked to introduce it, calling that a 'balanced' presentation."

Both these allegations were invented by the Attorney General's office after the Federal trial. They are lies that contradict the testimony and evidence given in court.

There was no reference to when or where these alleged statements were made because there was none.

ACTING ATTORNEY GENERAL'S OPINION*

In their appeal to the 2nd Circuit the defendants argued that the opinion should have been allowed as evidence despite the fact that the charges of violations of State Statutes and Division regulations were dropped. As a result, Blaine was never questioned about it during the trial, and he spent *zero* time discussing the composition of the Board or the opinion.

This did not stop the Attorney General's office from stating in its appeal that "THE PLAINTIFF SPENT A CONSIDERABLE AMOUNT OF TIME TESTIFYING AND ARGUING TO THE JURY THAT THE BOARD WAS NOT 'DULY CONSTITUTED' BECAUSE IT DID NOT HAVE THE FULL COMPLIMENT OF FIVE MEMBERS." And in a footnote, "...HE SHOULD NOT HAVE MADE HIS BALD STATEMENTS MALIGNING THE BOARD'S COMPOSITION."

The attorneys in the Attorney General's office who wrote this invented what occurred at trial. All they had to do was read the trial transcript for the truth. The statements are fabrications and a further example of their total disregard for the truth. As officers of the Court their behavior was in this writer's opinion disgraceful. As public officers of the Court their statements are even more unfathomable.

---

*The State Statutes required the Gaming Policy Board to have a quorum of 4 to take any action. The acting Attorney General's opinion stretched credibility by saying that 3 members instead of 4 could act as the Board, and then in a footnote extended the 3 to 2. They had no need for the opinion since the violations of State Statutes were not being adjudicated. They should have been ashamed of this sloppy piece of work that Assistant Attorney General Richard Sheridan admitted he wrote and Acting Attorney General Clarine Nardi Riddle signed. It was dated May 1, 1989, two weeks before Blaine was given an order to lie to the Board. How convenient.

SUMMARY OF CRUCIAL ERRORS BY DEFENDANTS IN OPPOSITION TO PETITION TO U.S. SUPREME COURT

Richard Blumenthal, Attorney General of Connecticut
Aaron S. Bayer, Deputy Attorney General
Robert F. Vacchelli, Counsel of Record, Assistant Attorney General
Gregory T. D'Auria, Assistant Attorney General

1. Lewis was a High-Ranking Policy-Making Official.
2. Lewis was ordered to present the "Division's Views".
3. Hickey's order was a lawful agency policy.
4. Lewis threatened to obstruct the process, Lewis expressed the intention to criticize publicly a change in the lottery game, and Lewis threatened to denounce the proposed Lotto game change publicly during the presentation to the Gaming Policy Board.
5. Lewis refused to promote the change.
6. Lewis' position, if followed, would have brought all Board business to a halt.

OPPOSITON TO SUPREME COURT PETITION
QUESTIONS PRESENTED

1. "Did the United States Court of Appeals correctly rule that a high-ranking, policy-making state employee does not have a First Amendment right to refuse his agency head's directive to promote a lawful agency policy concerning making a change in

a state-run lottery game?"

This, the only question posed by the defendants, is a repetition of the errors submitted to and accepted by the 2nd Circuit Court of Appeals:

Lewis was not a high-ranking, policy-making state employee. The Executive Director and the members of the Gaming Policy Board were the people appointed by the Governor to make policy. They were the Policymakers. Lewis was a manager and was the head of the lottery unit, one of seven units in the Division.

It was not a lawful agency policy. The policy could not become a lawful agency policy until the Board had voted for it. It was Lewis' duty and part of his job to present his analysis to the Board so that they could make an informed decision. They could accept or reject Lewis' analysis, but it would be up to them to vote and decide policy.

Lewis did not refuse to promote the change if it became lawful agency policy. He stated that he would implement the game if it became a lawful decision. He stated this clearly both to Hickey and to the Board members. He refused to *propose* the change in a favorable, positive manner, because that would have been a lie and a breach of the public trust. His offer to give the pros and cons, the possible advantages of a change as well as the possible dangers of the change, was rejected. He was fired for refusing to lie.

Page 1 (lines 5-13) "The Court of Appeals' decision in this case, entirely consistent with years of precedent established by this Court, stands for the utterly unremarkable proposition that a high-level, policy-making employee does not have a right to publicly criticize, undermine or refuse to implement a policy decision made by his agency head, and at the same time retain his job, serving at the pleasure of that agency head."

Lewis did not undermine or refuse to implement the change in lotto. It was his duty to present his opinions to the GPB and the Legislature's Public Safety Committee. He stated at trial and before the Board that he would implement the game should it be approved. After the order to lie, he made no public statements until he was put on leave.

The agency head (Hickey) could not make policy without a vote of the Board.

Lewis did not serve at the pleasure of his agency head, Hickey. He served at the pleasure of Hickey and the Board, as stated even by the defendants on page 1, lines 20-21, the very next paragraph.

P 2 (lines 7-9) "This would make it more difficult to win, but would also result in more roll-overs and, therefore, larger jackpots for winners."

The defendants wrote this in 1999 despite the fact that the change in the game in 1989 was responsible for such a dramatic decline in jackpots, sales and revenues.

P 2 (lines 9-12) "As head of the Division, Hickey bore the responsibility for the agency's performance."

When General Instrument became the new vendor despite Lewis' advice, and the game immediately crashed, in May 1988, the Division and General Instrument tried to blame the drop in sales on the lotto game Lewis had designed. Now they wanted Lewis to tell the Board he was in favor of a game change so that they could blame him again should the new design fail. Better still Lewis would be fired for disobeying an order if he refused to lie. Lewis knew he was being set up to bear the responsibility for the agency's bad performance, not Hickey.

P 2 (lines 14-15) "All other Unit Heads and the Lottery contractor agreed with the change, but Lewis did not."

Certainly the Lottery contractor agreed. It was their idea in order to put the blame on the game rather than taking responsibility for their disaster. The task of their rebuilding every terminal in the state was not completed until April 1989, almost one year later.

There was no evidence to support Hickey's claim that all other Unit Heads agreed with the change. Lewis knew this to be false.

P 2 (lines 28-29) "(Lewis's positon, if followed, would have brought all Board business to a halt.)"

Business would have continued as usual with no new actions until the Board was increased to at least four members. The state legislature had wisely decided this.

p 2 (note) "He clung to this belief despite a formal legal opinion of the state Attorney General specifically concluding that the Board could act notwithstanding the vacancies."

Lewis was not informed of the opinion when he was given the order. He learned of it during the Loudermill hearing conducted on May 24, 1989.

The opinion, signed by an acting Attorney General, was only an opinion. Even so, the opinion argued that 3 members could constitute a quorum and a footnote reduced the number to 2. The Connecticut Statute specifically requires a quorum of 4 to pass any action. The "formal legal opinion" does not constitute law. It is rather odd that Hickey did not inform Lewis of the opinion at the time of the order when Lewis questioned the legality of the Board.

P 3 (lines 14-16) "on the contrary, Lewis' denunciation of the Lotto change during its presentation would have defied not only a policy decision properly made by the agency head,......"

Lewis only wanted to give the pros and cons. He never threatened to denounce the Lotto change.

The defendants now admit that Lewis was not a policymaker, but they still fail to accept the role of the Board in policy decisions.

P 3 (lines 20-21) "Properly presenting and implementing the new Lotto game was part of his job as the Lottery Chief,...."

Properly presenting his own analysis based on his knowledge and experience was part of his job. That constituted his value to the Division and the state. It was for the policymakers to evaluate his input and make the decision. The record is clear on his willingness to implement the change if approved. His value to the Division was greater than that of a parrot.

P 4 (Line 30) – p 5 (line 4) "This conclusion resulted from a proper and routine application of the Pickering test, which balances the interests of the employee, as a citizen, in commenting upon matters of public concern against the interests of the state, as an employer, in promoting the efficiency of the public services it performs through its employees."

In this case, Lewis did not speak. Had his free speech not been violated, that speech would have been in the interests of the state, as history has shown.

P 5 (lines 18-19) "But the petitioner's threats to obstruct the process....."

Lewis never threatened to obstruct the process. His statements to the Board and his testimony at trial are the exact opposite of the above. This is another lie by the defendants, not supported by any evidence because there was none.

P 6 (lines 19-22) "In this case there was a strong showing of potential disruption where the Lottery chief expressed the intention to criticize publicly a change in a lottery game, posing an obvious risk to the success of the game."

Again, Lewis never threatened to publicly criticize the change in the lottery game. The defendants repeatedly use this lie to argue for a potential disruption that never existed.

P 7 (II) "The Court of Appeals Correctly Ruled Consistent With This Court's Precedent, That The Court, Not The Jury, Must Apply The *Pickering* Balancing Test."

The District Court made it clear, in the absence of the jury, that if it had to apply the Pickering balance test, it would decide in favor of Lewis. Letting the jury decide favored the defendants by giving them a second chance. The District Court felt that the law was "amorphous' on this question, and the court's decision helped, not hurt the defendants.

THE FINAL YEAR

Blaine had passed out the previous December when I was close enough to ease his fall, but he had immediately regained consciousness. I called his neurologist who told me to call his cardiologist. The cardiologist who was covering for Blaine's regular cardiologist was not concerned. Our last nightmare began in March 2000 with Blaine's routine visit to see his regular cardiologist. He was concerned enough to do not only a routine EKG, but to have Blaine wear a holter for 24 hours. The holter, which gave the doctor a running EKG for the 24 hours, indicated that Blaine needed a pacemaker. Another cardiologist whose specialty was the electrical aspects of the heart was consulted, and after testing Blaine to see if ventricular arrhythmias could be induced, a decision to give Blaine an ICD (implantable cardiovert defibrillator) was made. He would have a pacemaker and defibrilator all in one unit. He would be protected from both long intervals between heartbeats as well as fast, dangerous ventricular arrhythmias. The ICD was implanted on April 27, at Yale-New Haven Hospital. The procedure went well and only one overnight in the hospital was required.

In June, Blaine went into heart failure and was again hospitalized at Yale-New Haven for a week. Even though he had been in constant atrial fibrilation since his by-pass surgery in November 1995, and had done very well, the feeling was that the atrial fibrilation and the ICD were not compatible. Two cardioversions to put his heart into a sinus rhthym failed to last. He was put on a drug called amiodorone to help ensure a successful cardioversion. When Blaine began having problems with his balance I became alarmed and called the specialist. Even though I tried I must have failed to convey the severity of the problem. It was less than one more week before his hospital date for what we hoped would be a successful cardioversion. Seeing that he was having problems I would walk with my hands on his belt with every step he took. He liked to have breakfast before dressing, so on that terrible day, June 30, I was just behind him on the stairway going up to breakfast. When he tripped and fell forward, the tie on his bathrobe was useless. Despite the fall, he seemed okay except for a sore thigh. There was no swelling, no bruising, and no pain in the hip. How lucky we were, I thought.

Three days later, July 3, when halfway down the stairway, retiring for the evening, he could no longer stand. I managed to get him onto the bed by using a chair with casters. He had a Yale-New Haven Hospital appointment on July 6 for another cardioversion. We finally decided to get an ambulance to take us to Yale-New Haven. It was in the very early hours of the morning of July 4, Blaine's 80th birthday, that he was admitted. X-rays showed that he needed a half-hip replacement. Because he had been on coumadin to thin his blood, the orthopedic surgeon had to wait until July 10 to do the surgery. While we were waiting for the surgery to be done I requested that his neurologist be called in. The staff neurologists checked his blood and found an alarmingly high level of phenobarb. This finally explained the problems he had had with balance causing his fall. Blaine had been on phenobarb due to a simple partial seizure disorder developed after his May '92 cerebral hemorrhage. Unfortunately no one had realized that the drug, amiodorone, had interacted and increased his blood level of phenobarb.

Blaine's hip surgery was successful but he ended up in the cardiac Intensive Care Unit with heart problems. Watching the monitors with his fast pulses and low blood pressures was frightening, but after several days the numbers improved and he was released from the ICU to the regular cardiology floor. The hip surgery meant great care in his lying position in bed. He not only had to keep his leg aligned with his hip and not bend beyond 90 degrees, but he had to wear a special "podus" boot on his foot. He had developed a drop-foot during the surgery (damage to the peronial nerve) which caused the toes to drop. I was stunned to see the bed soars he had developed resulting from the necessity of lying on his back in one position. The more important concern was making sure his heart was stable and that his hip healed.

By July 21, Blaine was ready to leave the hospital but was so weak that he could not stand by himself, even with a walker. We went to a rehab facility in North Haven, where he received physical therapy. Unlike the hospital, which had provided me with a cot in his room so that I could stay with him around the clock, the rehab facility let me stay, but I had to make due with sleeping on a two-person settee. I was delighted as long as I could be with him. I would wash and dress him, help feed him, take him by wheelchair to the physical therapy room, and take part in his therapy. By the 28th of July, I felt he had improved enough so that I could take him home. Even though the staff at both the hospital and the rehab facility had been great, Blaine was thrilled to go home. We left the facility on July 29, and we were so happy that even my backing our car into a fire hydrant, on leaving, did not dampen our spirits.

At home Blaine had a visiting nurse come twice a week and a physical therapist come three times a week. The physical therapy was even better than what he had received at the rehab center. It was one on one and a more concentrated effort. His doctors had the lab send someone once a week to draw blood so that all his levels could be checked and medications modified as necessary. It was good to have the visiting nurse check him out and take charge of the extensive attention needed for caring for his bed soars. I would take his blood pressure and pulse several times a day as I had since he came home from the hospital from his original heart attack and cerebral hemorrhage in May 1992. Blaine's recovery was going well.

By the end of August Blaine's weight started to increase despite an increase in his diuretic. There were crackles on the right side of his chest and he was either in heart failure again or maybe pneumonia or a bronchial infection. The X-ray was inconclusive. On September 1, both a covering cardiologist and his primary care physician agreed to put him on antibiotics and increase his diuretic. By September 4, Labor day, it was apparent that his condition was worsening. I called the cardiologist and drove him to Yale-New Haven where he was admitted for heart failure. The staff was fantastic and made Blaine feel that it was a homecoming.

The nurses were very special and we were grateful. By the 8th, he was able to come home again. The nurse's, physical therapist's and lab visits all resumed. All again was going well. Besides working with his therapists and me, he kept his mind occupied with reading his newsmagazines and newspapers, and listening to talk radio. He never lost his quick wit or wonderful sense of humor.

By the beginning of October, Blaine was walking alone with the walker. He even walked with a cane with a good stride and arm swinging with the therapist or me. I was so proud of him. I had been getting up with him in the middle of the night for several months, but now he was so secure with the walker that we felt it would be safe to let him get up by himself. He had been doing this for a week when the horrible accident happened.

It was 12:15 am on the 9th of October when Blaine got up to go to the bathroom. Seconds after he entered the bathroom I heard a loud crash. I jumped out of bed and was by his side in a few seconds. Blaine had fallen back and his head had hit the flagstone floor in the hall, just inches away from both the carpeted bedroom and carpeted bathroom. His head was in a pool of blood and blood was coming out his left ear. He was conscious and wanted to get up. He kept asking me, "What happened, Tina?" I was in a state of panic and shook uncontrollably. I saw no cuts for there were none. I put a towel under his head and called 911. I kept telling him that everything was going to be all right and he was not to worry. I ran upstairs to turn on the lights and open the door so that the police and ambulance personnel could come right in when they arrived. I then ran back to Blaine and while talking to him and trying to reassure him I threw on some clothes. It was only later that I realized there was blood everywhere, on my nightgown, the telephone, the wall switch, the walls. He stayed conscious and coherent during the ambulance ride to the Hartford Hospital. He was even conscious for a short time in the emergency room. He kept asking me repeatedly what had happened which indicated that he had passed out. If he had lost his balance, he would have remembered. I told him that he was in the hospital and that he was going to be all right. His very last words were so typical of Blaine, not feeling sorry for himself but worrying about me. "Poor Tina" he said. Maybe someday I'll be able to stop crying when I think of it. The bleeding was so intense that he lost consciousness. A cat scan showed a blood clot on the brain and I was told by the neurosurgeon on call that night that his chances were not good but he might survive with emergency surgery. I did not have to think twice about the surgery. I wanted to give Blaine every possible chance.

At 3 in the morning when Blaine went into the operating room, I went to the family waiting room at the neurosurgical ICU. I was horrified at the possibility of losing Blaine and I was so shaken that despite the hour, I phoned my brother, John and told him what had happened. He came right then from Barkhamsted and sat with me through the night. I felt so grateful for his company. When the neurosurgeon came to the waiting room, he told us that Blaine had tolerated the surgery quite well. I was elated.

After the first few days Blaine seemed to be coming out of it. He moved his feet and arms a bit and was responsive even though he never spoke. He had tubes into his nose and mouth and was connected to a ventilator as well as a swan catheter (it goes through the chambers of your heart) as well as an arterial line into his groin and all of this connected to monitors. He also had numerous IV's. He developed pneumonia and heart failure and a follow-up cat scan showed there had been some additional bleeding at the sight of the original head surgery. Even though antibiotics were given for the pneumonia and the heart became reasonably stable, Blaine was never to regain consciousness.

He had recovered from so many earlier health problems and I kept hoping that he would recover again. I could not give up. He had a G tube into his stomach for nutrition. When that was not successful he went to radiology where he received a G J tube which also went into his intestine. He had to be on dopomine to keep his blood pressure from dropping. IV's were no longer possible so a triple lumen had to be used for all his medications and nutrition. His face and his complexion looked so good. If he would only wake up, I felt all would eventually be all right.

In his final week he had developed a total bowel blockage. The day before he died, I was told by Dr. Brady, my cancer surgeon in whom I had great confidence, that his intestine had been perforated and that he needed major colon surgery and would require a colostomy. It was a painful and difficult procedure under normal conditions. She strongly advised against it. I was also told he would never leave the ICU because of his dependence on dopomine. I was told that his chances of waking up were zero. But it was only the need for surgery that destroyed my hope. As I tried to sleep in the lounge that night, the very lounge where I had spent most of my previous 7 weeks, I lost all hope and feared that I might cause Blaine to suffer needlessly.

The next morning, November 28, I called my brother again and he came into the ICU to stay with me. After he arrived, Blaine's defibrillator was deactivated and the dopomine was stopped. He was put on morphine just in case he had any pain. It was before noon, at about 11 am. I watched the monitors as I had for the past 7 weeks. This time it was with despair and indescribable misery that I watched him slowly die. The nurses and aides all came into the room one a time and, with tears in their eyes, they all hugged me. I was so grateful for all the kindness they showed me and the gentleness with which they treated Blaine. I held his hand and kissed him. I told him how much I loved him. I told him how sorry I was. Only God knows if he heard me. Only God knows whether the doctors were right when they told me he had not suffered. He took his last breath at 5:40 PM.

Blaine and I only spoke of death once, very briefly. I suggested we both be cremated and our ashes dispersed together. He smiled and with a twinkle in his eye he told me that was a great idea. My suggestion of the ocean appealed to him because we had worked so hard to build our dream cottage there, but anywhere was all right with him. I am so grateful that we had our brief conversation. Our ashes will be dispersed together and we will be together in spirit for eternity.

ACKNOWLEDGEMENTS

I want to express my gratitude and Blaine's gratitude to William S. Rogers, Esq. for representing Blaine for the many years of his legal battle for justice. The legal battle waged by the Attorney General's office, at taxpayer's expense, created an unbelievable and time-consuming amount of work. Blaine's confidence in Bill's intelligence, ability and character were in no small part responsible for Blaine's ability to fight back from the devastation to his health caused by the stress and many injustices of those years. The victory in the Connecticut Superior Court in December 1989 with Judge Samuel Freed presiding, and the victory by the unanimous decision of the jury in Blaine's trial in Federal District Court with Judge Thomas P. Smith presiding were a vindication, despite the fact that both were reversed. The jury watched and heard the defendants and Blaine, heard the evidence and discerned the truth. They were not fooled. We were grateful to all the jurors, always attentive, and Judge Smith for enabling Blaine to have a fair trial.

I would also like to express my gratitude to my brother, John G. Lizzi, who was always ready and willing to help us. From installing grab bars in the bath tub to running errands to staying with me during Blaine's emergency brain surgery and again during Blaine's final hours, John was always there. It would take pages to list all his good deeds. Blaine felt very fortunate having such a willing and capable brother-in-law.

I would like to thank all of Blaine's doctors, nurses and staff both at Yale-New Haven and the Hartford Hospital for all the years of good medical attention he received. We always felt they were doing their best, and their warmth and caring attitude were very helpful during difficult times.

I could never have imagined the kindness and support that I was to receive from friends and neighbors when Blaine died. They shopped, cooked meals, and brought me baskets of food, flowers, and books on grieving. They listened to my sobbing and gave me comfort. They understood my need to talk about Blaine. I shall always be grateful.

NOTES

APPENDIX

INTERDEPARTMENTAL MESSAGE
STO-201 REV 7/86
Stock No. 6938-051-01)

STATE OF CONNECTICUT

Obtain "STATE EMPLOYEE SUGGESTION" forms from, and send your ideas to: Employee's Suggestion Awards Program, 165 Capital Avenue Hartford, Ct. 06106.

	NAME, TITLE	DATE
To	Theodore Faraci, Chief of Procurement	December 4,
	AGENCY, ADDRESS	
	Department of Administrative Service	

	NAME, TITLE	TELEPHONE
From	J. Blaine Lewis, Jr., Lottery Chief	2912
	AGENCY, ADDRESS	
	Division of Special Revenue	

Subject: On-Line Lottery Bid

In accordance with our discussion on December 2, I have assembled all of my thoughts on subject bid.

The total dollar difference between the low bidder (General Instrument) and the next lowest (GTECH) is approximately $11,000,000 for the five-year period or an average of $2.2 million per year. On an absolute basis, this is a substantial sum. However, it should be viewed in context.

The average yearly on-line lottery sales for the five-year period is expected to be $460,000,000. Since the lottery nets approximately 40%, the average yearly profit will be $184,000,000. Therefore, the theoretical saving is less than 1.2% of the expected profit. On each of three recent exceptional days (10/27/87, 10/29/87, 10/30/87), the average daily net profit for the on-line lottery system was $2.3 million which is in excess of this theoretical annual saving. It is my opinion, that viewed in context, the price difference is minimal.

In addition to comparing the bid prices, we must also compare the two bidders:

GTECH

1. GTECH is the world's foremost on-line lottery supplier serving 28 jurisdictions worldwide, 21 of these are full-service contracts such as ours.

2. GTECH has approximately 40,000 on-line lottery terminals in service approximately 18,000 of which are the type which they would supply to us.

3. The principal business of GTECH is on-line lotteries.

GENERAL INSTRUMENT

1. General Instrument is a highly diversified Fortune 500 Company. Its on-line lottery activities account for a microscopic proportion of its business activity and very probably make a negative contribution to corporate earnings.

-1-

2. General Instrument has in service appro nately 1200 terminals of the type they propose to us. These 1200 terminals, however, are not identical to the ones proposed to us and are in a very tranquil environment with a terminal transaction rate of approximately $1/8^{th}$ of the terminal transaction rate in Connecticut.

3. General Instrument at one time was the leader in on-line lotteries. Today, on-line lotteries amount to a tiny, apparently money-losing, segment of the business.

4. General Instrument has no satisified customers in the United States for this type of lottery operation.

5. General Instruments only customer (Missouri) will not release documents relating to their performance because they "relate to legal actions, causes of action or litigation involving a public governmental body and confidential or privileged communications between the Commission and its attorneys under Section 610.021(1)".

6. General Instrument was rejected by the New Jersey Lottery even though they were the low bidder and the incumbent.

7. General Instrument was rejected by the Ohio Lottery even though they were the low bidder and the incumbent.

8. General Instrument has never changed over a live system – they have always been the outgoing party.

9. The "phantom ticket" situation which occurred on the General Instrument system at the New Jersey Lottery was appalling and would be unacceptable in Connecticut.

10. General Instrument's proposal to us contained an unsolicited statement about "an unblemished record of integrity" which is untrue. Records of Superior Court of New Hampshire show Amtote employee guilty of tampering with lottery system.

11. General Instrument's proposal to us contained the statement:

    "If any part of the work is to be subcontracted, General Instrument will provide the Division with a description of the subcontracting organization and the proposed contractual arrangements. General Instrument also understands and will comply with the requirement that all such contractual arrangements must have the prior approval of the Deputy Commissioner, Bureau of Purchases and the Division."

    General Instrument did not notify us that they planned to subcontract the manufacturing of the terminals and sent us information on the subcontractor only after we learned about the proposed subcontracting and requested information about the sub-contractor.

-2-

149

12. As mentioned earlier, General Instrument was at one time the acknowledged leader in the field and by 1986 was essentially out of the on-line lottery business. The obvious question is "why?" I believe that the answer is poor service. Documentary evidence is not often readily available on situations such as this, however, the report of the hearing officer for the Division of Purchase and Property for the State of New Jersey dated April 26, 1984 is revealing. The report is authored by Burton Weltman, Esq. who was the hearing officer for the Division of Purchase and Property in the State of New Jersey for the protest hearing held to evaluate complaints of unsuccessful bidders after GTECH was awarded the contract to replace Amtote as the on-line vendor for the New Jersey Lottery. Following are excerpts from this report:

Page 12- lines 4-6

"The Committee essentially determined that Amtote's past record in New Jersey was such that the Committee felt Amtote's risk of poor performance was too great."

Page 13, paragraph 2

"Based on this evidence, I find that: (1) Amtote failed to fulfill some critical promises that it made during the course of the existing contract, and in particular as to the installation of "fast lotto;" (2) the comparative statistics show that Amtote's equipment has a breakdown rate of 2 to 3 times that of GTECH's equipment, and that Amtote's repair service is less prompt than GTECH's; and , (3) the opinions of lottery officials from other jurisdictions are generally more favorable to GTECH than to Amtote. And, I conclude that evidence is sufficient to sustain the Committee's recommendations as to Amtote's bids."

Page 38 and paragraph 1 of page 39

"(ii) With respect to the anecdotal evidence about Amtote's performance in New Jersey, I find that the stories of "fast-lotto" and of the OMR's seem to represent significant, and inadequately justified, departures from legitimate expectations of performance which Amtote itself created. Amtote cannot, and did not, offer as an excuse for its performance on these two items any claim that the Lottery set unreasonable time tables for implementation. Amtote promised these items at certain times, and then did not meet its own time-tables. I find reasonable the Committee's testimony that, in the lottery business, the lottery must be able reasonably to rely on its vendor and its vendor's promises. In turn, I find reasonable the Committee's concern about an incumbent vendor which did not even meet its own timetables.

Furthermore, I find creditable the Committee's data as to dilatory service calls by Amtote. Even accepting Amtote's analysis of the figures, I find that the Committee could

-3-

reasonably conclude that the service record was unacceptable, and pointed toward a "loss of priority" and loss of reliability as to performance. While Amtote may be correct in its claim that the liquidated damages clause in the new contract should help minimize any service delays by the vendor, the Committee could reasonably conclude that the fact that these service delays existed under the current contract may point to incompatible attitudes toward lottery operations between Amtote and the New Jersey Lottery. That is, even under the current contract, all parties make more money when terminals operate full-time. The New Jersey Lottery seems most concerned to maximize current revenue and future growth, by providing the highest level service. Based on the record, the Committee might reasonably conclude that Amtote does not share the same zeal as the Lottery.

Likewise, I find reasonable the Committee's concern that Amtote never found the cause of the misprinted tickets. Beyond the fact that these misprinted tickets adversely impact on the credibility of the Lottery, the Committee could reasonably see Amtote's failure in this matter as cumulative evidence, along with services record, of "loss of priority" and reliability."

Since there is on the record a memorandum dated November 23, 1987 and a report dated November 24, 1987 from the Assessment team consisting of Gordon Partridge, Robert Mitchell, Donald J. Maloney and Brian Gorman which appear, on the surface at least, to conflict with my views I feel obliged to comment on these documents.

The memo states "we feel that the G.I. bid offering is a viable offering to the state with no negative risk factors detected in our day-long visit"

The report states, "Based on the observations in Hunt Valley, the committee has decided the Division will realize no negative risk if the bid is awarded to General Instrument at this time. Any existing risk factors would be applicable to any vendor".

The key phrases in these documents are "detected in our day-long visit" and "Based on the observations in Hunt Valley".

Since the assessment team has relied so heavily, if not solely, on information obtained in one-day at Hunt Valley, it occurred to me that I should determine, at least approximately, what percentage of that information was independently verified and what percentage was taken at face value from General Instrument. I put that question to Mr. Maloney and Mr. Gorman. Mr. Maloney told me he could not answer that question. Mr. Gorman informed me that it would take a great deal of analysis to answer that question. The following example will illustrate how important it is to have this question answered. Page 4 of the report attempts to explain the New Jersey Lottery data base error as follows: "This was caused by faulty terminals misprinting tickets..." and "The terminals were checked and proven faulty because of age..." Since the assessment team had no way of independently verifying this allegation, it obviously falls into the category of information taken from General Instrument at face value. On the same subject, Mr. John Kirkland of General Instrument testified at the New Jersey hearing.

"I would like to make a comment on misprinted tickets, which was a discussion of this morning.

The good will in question by Mr. Mule' was, indeed, acknowledged to have been paid for by Amtote. In any system operation of this size, scope, magnitude, the troubleshooting, if you will, of hardware or software related problems can be a very tedious event. The time period that was identified from 1980 to 1983 to resolve, if you will, the problem in total, there was never a point in time during that period that the problem was able to be replicated by ourselves in a laboratory environment; this was regularly made known to the Lottery, that the problem was still being looked into on a very regular basis. Everytime they wanted, by request, to settle claims for payment of these tickets in question, we used that data and documentation to further analyze the problem. Since the last field terminal firmware change there have not been any claims subsequent to that change that I am aware of..."

The assessment team was told in Hunt Valley that the problem was due to terminals proven faulty because of age. However, the Hearing Officer in New Jersey was told by General Instrument that they had tried unsuccessfully for 3 years to replicate the problem in a laboratory environment. Surely a laboratory could make a determination in less than 3 years if worn out terminals were really the problem.

In view of the foregoing, I suggest that the memo of November 23 and the report of November 24 be heavily discounted.

Conclusion

As mentioned earlier, the theoretical saving is minimal when viewed in context. A 1.2% reduction in sales due to poor service will eliminate the theoretical saving. We should not lose sight of the fact that the lottery is equivalent in earning capacity to #143 on the Fortune 500 list and is the state's fourth largest source of income.

It may well be that General Instrument could correct its problems and regain its former position in the industry but I do not believe that the Connecticut State Lottery should be the guinea pig.

Based on 20 years' experience in business as an electrical engineer and 14 years experience in the lottery business, 10 of which were in on-line lotteries, it is my opinion that sound business judgement dictates that the award should be made to GTECH.

cc: Orlando P. Ragazzi

-5-

Interdepartment Message

O-201 REV. 11/81 STATE OF CONNECTICUT

?ck No. 693R-051-01)

SAVE TIME: *Handwritten messages are acceptable.*

Use carbon if you really need a copy. If typewritten, ignore faint lines.

	NAME	TITLE	DATE
To	John W. Otterbein	Deputy Commissioner	12/9/87
	AGENCY Administration	ADDRESS	

	NAME	TITLE	TELEPHONE
From	T.A. Faraci, CPPO	Chief of Procurement	3280
	AGENCY Procurement	ADDRESS	

SUBJECT: On Line Lottery; Bid 812-A-4-1959-C

I believe I have studied all the evidence presented for the award of the above contract, to such a degree that I can state an award recommendation.

I think it is in the best interests of the State and in keeping with sound business judgement to award bid 812-A-4-1959-C to G. Tech, our present contractor.

SP-7A, our standard bid and contract terms and conditions states the following as Criteria for making an award:

> P22 "Award will be made to the lowest, responsible, qualified Bidder. The quality of articles or services to be supplied, their conformity with the specifications, their suitability to the requirements of the State, and the delivery terms will be taken into consideration in making the award." (emphasis added)

It appears that General Instrument may have met most of the above criteria. The proposed terminal to be used seems to be "state of the art" and capable of performing the required functions for our on-line system. The visit to GI's subcontractor for terminal manufacturer was impressive to the State's representative. However, it must be pointed out that GI, gave no indication in its bid that anyone would perform the terminal manufacturing operation other than itself.

The listing of subcontractors was a bid requirement. In prior years, I believe GI manufactured its own terminals.

The visit to GI's facility in Hunt Valley, Maryland also impressed the State representatives that made the trip. GI does have a self imposed schedule for gearing up to our on line contract and reportedly is near completion of the software to run the system. The software is probably the most integral part of any on-line system from a technical standpoint.

Given this information, other technical factors, and its pricing structure on the bid proposal, GI is seemingly the lowest responsible bidder. However, I think SP-7A also allows the Deputy Commissioner of Purchases to consider other factors that relate to a bidders total qualification before making an award decision.

Paragraph 25 reads as follows:

> "A Bidder, if requested, must be prepared to
> present evidence of experience, ability
> service facilities and financial standing
> necessary to meet satisfactorily the
> requirements set forth or implied in the
> bid."

It is in the context of this paragraph that I believe GI's bid contains serious
reservations which requires further research in order that a sound and practical
business decision can be concluded. Let us review some of the subjects referred
to in, Paragraph 25.

a. Financial standing- It is irrefutable that GI's on-line division
is the weakest link in the company. GI's annual report pegs
this division as a money loser in and of itself. It may be
true that GI, the Corporation, intends to financially back
its weak division, but if the division continues its weak
revenue producing performance, how long can or will
Corporation continue to support such an operation? Even
assurances from GI's chairman of the Board to support
the on-line division financially, and his agreement not to
sell off the operation cannot be construed as a guarantee
should the Board of Directors of GI conclude that a departure
from such a guarantee is in the best interests of the Corporation.

b. Experience and ability- It has been discussed that the
State should not consider GI's "ancient history." This
"history" cannot be disputed as GI has fallen from the
leader in the on-line lottery industry to the bottom. There
must exist concrete reasons for this rapid decline, although
it is doubtful that the State will ever learn them. However,
to place the lottery's best revenue producing operation in
the hands of such a supplier, is definitely not in the States
best interests. If we consider, GI's performance in New Jersey
documented by official testimony, and the fact that in New
Jersey and Ohio GI was both the low bidder and the incumbent
contractor but still was not awarded a contract, we can conclude
that these actions do not speak well of GI's ability as a vendor
to fully satisfy its customers.

If we discount GI's failures in New Jersey and Ohio as never having existed or
as "ancient history", on what can the State base GI's experience? GI's only current
domestic customer is the State of Missouri. This was a start-up type system that
did not exist prior to GI's selection as the contractor. Since the State of Missouri
will not release pertinent information about GI's contract performance, we have
no experience on which to judge GI's ability to perform. It may be safe to assume
that Missouri's refusal to release information indicates the State is not totally
satisfied with GI's performance.

Since Missouri is GI's only customer reference, does the State of Connecticut
wish to gamble a smoothly running system that is nearly twice the size in terminals
and 8 times the terminal transaction rate on a contractor with extremely limited
experience?

APPENDIX

In conclusion, if GI's performances in Ohio and New Jersey are considered, I do not think GI is a qualified bidder as defined by SP-7A, paragraph 22.

If GI's "ancient history" good and bad is not considered, then GI is a bidder with severly limited experience and ability and therefore, should be disqualified based on the points outlined in paragraph 25 of SP-7A.

Personally, I believe GI desparately wants the Connecticut contract to use as a springboard to get back into the full swing of the on-line business. Given the current size and success of our on-line lottery an award of this contract to GI is in GI's best interests and not those of the State. Clearly SP-7A allows for the rejection of any bid if the "best interests of the State will be served." It is my professional opinion that GI's bid does not serve the best interests of the State.

MEMORANDUM

TO: Orlando P. Ragazzi, Executive Director
FROM: Albert S. Acayan, Unit Head/L&IA
DATE: 25 April 1988
SUBJECT: Initial Systems Acceptance Testing
          GIC On Line System

Please be informed that the On-Line system made available to the Division for testing appears not to have been ready at the time of presentation. Even GIC personnel verbally admitted that their system had not been debugged and that they were relying on my staff to find the bugs.

By contract, GIC was supposed to have been ready for the L&IA testers 12 April 1988 for the conversion phase of the testing. As it turned out, GIC was not ready for the Division until Thursday, 14 April 1988. Although the system was made available that day, processing errors were so numerous that that portion of the test was postponed and to date, GIC is still not ready for the Division's testing.

Switching to software testing, we have been frustrated by the system's inadequacies coupled with recurring errors. It certainly appears that correction of a problem brought to their attention causes other processes to become undone - and so on down the line. Please be reminded that the contract deadline for the Division's testing is 28 April 1988. Because of the discrepancies, we have been unable to go beyond the first weekly close-out.

My staff of testers have uncomplainingly tested in excess of the contract stipulated 9 hours per day. We even tested on a Sunday. For GIC to have the system available to us until midnight everyday for testing is very commendable. To expect my overworked staff to test from 8:00 a.m. until midnight would be taxing them physically and perhaps needlessly. After all, productivity does decline when fatigue starts setting in.

I ask you to reconsider your position on this and suggest that GIC spend those nighttime hours debugging and testing their system so that when Division testing resumes in the morning, we should expect fewer and fewer discrepancies.

I await your reply.

cc: W. T. Drakeley
     J. B. Lewis, Jr.
     E. J. Meder
     GIC File /

APPENDIX

STD-201 REV 7/86
(Stock No. 6938-037-01)

STATE OF CONNECTICUT

Obtain "STATE EMPLOYEE SUGGESTION" forms from, and send your
ideas to: Employee's Suggestion Awards Program, 165 Capitol Avenue
Hartford, Ct, 06106.

	NAME, TITLE	DATE
To	Orlando P. Ragazzi, Executive Director	May 5, 1988
	AGENCY, ADDRESS Division of Special Revenue	
	NAME, TITLE	TELEPHONE
From	J. Blaine Lewis, Jr., Lottery Chief	2912
	AGENCY, ADDRESS Division of Special Revenue	

Subject: On-line transition

In compliance with your decision to go live with General Instrument
on May 8, we have made the following arrangements:

1. Tapes and hard-copy reports will be picked up at GTECH
   at 4:00 a.m. on Sunday, May 8 and delivered to General Instrument
   at approximately 4:30 a.m. by a DOSR security officer.

2. Agents will be notified by Lottery on May 5 that the new system
   will become operational at 12:00 Noon on May 8.

   (This schedule gives GI their requested 6 hours for loading
   and leaves 1½ hours cushion.)

3. A press release will be issued explaining why the system will
   start at Noon instead of 6:00 a.m.

4. Our field representatives will be instructed by General Instrument
   on May 5 at 2:00 p.m. with regard to their support of
   General Instrument on May 8 and May 9.

I will cake this opportunity to advise you that it is my opinion that
we are exposing ourselves to considerable and unnecessary risk by
allowing General Instrument to go live on May 8.

I believe that we do not have sufficient indication that they are
ready.

JBL:r

157

MEMORANDUM

TO: Orlando P. Ragazzi, Executive Director
FROM: Albert S. Acayan, Unit Head/L&IA
DATE: 5 May 1988
SUBJECT: Initial System Acceptance Test of the General
           Instrument Corporation's On-Line System

As you may remember, in a meeting held in your office during the
early part of the contract negotiations with GIC, I was queried
as to the length of time I would require to conduct "L&IA's test"
of the system. Based on my knowledge of system tests but without
consultation with my staff, I had indicated two months. Subsequent to the meeting, I did consult with my staff and without
prompting from me, the response I received was for a test period
of not less than 60 days.

Notwithstanding, I was later approached and asked to give a best
guess estimate of time to conduct "L&IA's test" assuming testing
went well to which my response was 90 hours. These 90 hours were
then compressed to a two-week period of nine-hour workdays to
conduct what we in L&IA thought was "software testing" only. We
were then informed that these 90 hours were for all phases of
testing - load, software, and conversion. We actually went from
an initial request of two months for software testing to two
weeks for load, software, and conversion testing, two of which -
software and conversion - require user-controlled environments to
allow for the proper tracking of information through the system.

Again notwithstanding, GIC was not ready for conversion on April
12, 1988 as provided for in the contract. We commenced conversion testing April 14, 1988. Results were considered so unacceptable that conversion testing was discontinued and software testing commenced on April 15, 1988. It became obvious to us that
the debugging of the system, if any, had been kept to a minimum
and there was a heavy reliance on the Division's testing to bring
these "bugs" to light. The scope of our test was not intended
for debugging purposes - rather, it was to provide the Division
assurance to the extent that we were confident of the information
flow, balances, and amounts reflected in the various documents
generated by the system.

With the perseverance and dedication of some members of the L&IA
staff - Leona Scott, Deborah Joraskie, and Eric Meder, in particular - the unpleasant job of conducting the test in less than
acceptable conditions was performed. Based on the error level,
the types of errors encountered, and the continual recurrence of
errors already corrected, it became apparent that the contract
deadline date of April 28, 1988 for the conclusion of testing
would not be met. This was realized when a particular logical
day, which was a Wednesday (the day after a Daily & Play 4 draw,
a Lotto Draw and an accounting weekend) was repeated three times
- none of them right. The errors and discrepancies noted are

APPENDIX

well documented, copies of which can be made available if they
are needed.

The first "dry run conversion" was held on Sunday, 24 April 1988.
Reports from the converted data base were provided to the Division and were subsequently found to be out of balance with the
reports provided by the current vendor. For this exercise, the
tapes from GTech were delivered to GIC Sunday morning. The prin-
touts from GIC were released to the Division Monday evening.

On April 26, 1988, a meeting was held at the Division's Board
room that was attended by both Division and GIC staff. As was to
be expected, we were given the assurance that everything was
fixed and testing could resume but with extended timetables. The
Division, apparently, is allowed to conduct testing up to and
probably including implementation.

Testing resumed April 27, 1988, the fourth try of the first logical Wednesday. Although discrepancies were encountered, they
were either fixed on the fly or deemed as not material enough but
subject to being addressed May 9, 1988. The Division kept to its
revised schedule until Friday, April 29, 1988 when the error
level and types of errors encountered slowed us down, necessitat-
ing testing on a Sunday again. Software testing was concluded
this noon, May 5, 1988. Discrepancies that were brought to GIC's
attention - discrepancies considered material enough to severely
impact operations - were properly addressed by GIC. We hope.

The second "dry run conversion" was held that Sunday, May 1,
1988. GIC insisted that a bad reel of tape was transmitted to
them. Division copies of the tape were provided to them with the
same results. Finally, GTech personnel were called to provide a
third tape which was scrutinized to the nth degree before being
released to GIC. GIC also maintained that the third tape was incorrect. This posture was maintained by GIC until some 16 hours
after receipt of the first tapes when it was begrudgingly admitted that perhaps GIC was in error and the tapes were good -
all three sets of them. Notwithstanding, the Division did not
receive reports from this dry run until last evening, May 4,
1988.

With respect to the Division's "conversion test" L&IA was put on
standby by GIC relative to start time. We were called Monday
morning, May 2, 1988. We responded only to find out that they
were not ready. Initial reports were reviewed and discrepancies
were pointed out. Testing finally commenced on Wednesday, May 4,
1988. Target date for completion of this test is tomorrow,
Friday, May 6, 1988. It took three weeks to cycle through our

Orlando P. Ragazzi
5 May 1988
ISAT on GIC's On-Line System
Page 3

software test that had a very limited data base. Three days for successfully completing the conversion testing is asking for a miracle. It is a physical impossibility to get that accomplished at this late date. Discrepancies still exist.

There are still areas that remain untested or unconfirmed. Among these are:

1. Purging of GIC-generated winning tickets from the system one year after draw date

2. Purging of GTech-generated winning tickets from the system one year after draw date

3. Applied Payment Deposits (APD)

4. Free Play (later testing agreed upon)

5. Skip draw dates

It should be pointed out that certain critical areas that were tested and found incorrect and subsequently corrected have not been retested. Among these are:

1. Complete week end cycle including report generation

2. Lotto draw

3. Posting of agent adjustments

4. Agent invoicing

5. Pool Report procedures (Daily/Play 4)

Based on the above, I can not recommend the use of the GIC system by the Division. At the minimum, the system should be retested in its entirety to ensure that the areas addressed and corrected have not affected other processes. The system might run with minor discrepancies but there is very little confidence of this occurrence.

:aa

★ Every Idea Is A Link In The Chain of Progress ★
Send your Ideas to: *Employees' Suggestion Awards Program, 165 Capitol Ave., Hartford, 06115*

Interdepartment Message

STO-200 REV. 5-81 *(Stock No. 6938-050-01)*

SAVE TIME: *Handwritten messages are acceptable.*
Use carbon if you really need a copy. If typewritten, ignore faint lines.

	NAME	TITLE	DATE
To	Mr. J. Blaine Lewis, Jr.	Unit Chief/Lottery	May 6, 1988
	AGENCY	ADDRESS	
	Division of Special Revenue		

	NAME	TITLE	TELEPHONE
From	Orlando P. Ragazzi	Executive Director	566-2757
	AGENCY	ADDRESS	
	Division of Special Revenue		

SUBJECT

On-line transition

I am in receipt of your memo, same subject above, dated May 5, 1988.

Please respond in writing and elaborate the specifics of the following sentence contained in your memo:

> "I will take this opportunity to advise you that it is my opinion that we are exposing ourselves to considerable and unnecessary risk by allowing General Instrument to go live on May 8."

Thank you.

★ OPR:sja

SAVE TIME: *If convenient, handwrite reply to sender on this same sheet.*

**ⁱERDEPARTMENTAL
MESSAGE**
STD-201 REV. 7/86
(Stock No. 6938-031-01)

STATE OF CONNECTICUT

Obtain "STATE EMPLOYEE SUGGESTION" forms from, and send your
ideas to: Employee's Suggestion Awards Program, 165 Capitol Avenue
Hartford, Ct. 06106.

	NAME, TITLE	DATE
To	Orlando P. Ragazzi, Executive Director	May 6, 1988
	AGENCY, ADDRESS Division of Special Revenue	
From	NAME, TITLE J. Blaine Lewis, Jr., Lottery Chief	TELEPHONE 2912
	AGENCY, ADDRESS Division of Special Revenue	

Subject: Your memo of May 6, 1988

In my memo of May 5, 1988, I make the following statement:

"I will take this opportunity to advise you that it is
my opinion that we are exposing ourselves to considerable
and unnecessary risk by allowing General Instrument to
go live on May 8".

It was made for the following reasons:

1. General Instrument's extremely poor performance in our
   software tests.

2. General Instrument's poor performance in the conversion
   tests.

3. General Instrument's poor performance in our terminal tests.

4. As of today, they are still not ready to go on the EFT.

5. We could have extended the GTECH contract for 10 weeks to
   give General Instrument more time to get ready. I realize
   that there is the possibility that General Instrument would
   bring legal action in this event, however, I believe it is
   extremely unlikely that they would sue their only paying
   customer for lottery operation.

JBL:r

162

MEMORANDUM

TO: Orlando P. Ragazzi, Executive Director
FROM: Eric J. Meder, Assistant Unit Head/ L&IA
DATE: May 18, 1988

SUBJECT: Impact of Problems Experienced With GIC on Accounting
         Operations Within L&IA

You are already aware of all the unsatisfactory performance in-
cidences as of yesterday under the contract with GIC, therefore I
will not reiterate them. Rather, the purpose of this memorandum
is to inform you of the serious impact those and new problems
have created and will continue to create if not resolved immediately. The most serious are summarized as follows:

1. Unbalanced system reports have disallowed the continuity of
the normal accounting cycle (Wednesday morning to Tuesday night).
This has caused the inability to post correctly and/or completely
to the agents invoices for payments they may have made on last
week's business. As a most recent example that occurred this
morning, approximately 90% of the 143 manual postings made to
agents invoices for things such as cash advances, manual payments, and sales adjustments (necessary because of GI's foul-up)
were not reflected on the actual invoice those agents received
from the GI system. This has created many more incorrect invoices for agents and will require much effort on our part to
correct.

As of this morning, reports for Sunday May 8, 1988 were sent from
GI and appear to be ok. Through our continued efforts, im-
balances for Monday May 9, 1988 have been identified and shown to
GI. We are not yet in receipt of balanced reports for that day
or the following Tuesday and weeks' end.

I should point out that at the meeting of yesterday with GI, it
was represented to us that we had just received balanced reports
for May 8-10 including week end. Upon inspection of those
reports beginning with May 8, they were found to be identical to
those unbalanced reports we already had. It has become difficult to rely on anything that is represented to us.

Further to this point, we should be aware of the potential dis-
putes from agents which may result in administrative proceedings.
The Division's position at those proceedings will be quite
tenuous if we cannot rely on system information to support our
position.

2. For the week ending May 10, 1988 there was approximately $4.25
million due from agents that are on Auto-Pay (EFT). The State
should have been credited for that amount on Friday May 13, 1988
and one business day later should have had the funds available
for the State Treasurer's investment. These funds will not be

credited to the state until tomorrow which means the State has lost use of these funds for several days.

In addition, the collection of receipts for our manual pick-up agents has been several days late and has resulted in many discrepancies. Discrepancies resulted basically because agents are reluctant to pay an amount that appears incorrect. Unless we insist that GI rectify the discrepancies, my collection staff will be faced with a large volume of collection assignments that will be difficult to explain and/or collect.

3. As of this morning we received the first load of agent settlement envelopes. As a result of our audit findings on the settlements, there may be unknown problems yet to surface.

4. Operational confusion within GI relating to collections, in light of the numerous invoicing problems noted above, has presented a nightmarish condition in our offices. Agents don't know what to pay, the GI couriers don't know what they owe, therefore we are trying to handle a steady flow of calls from aggravated agents. I must admit that is very difficult for us to know exactly what certain agents owe because of compounded problems. We have not been able to correct the problems fast enough to keep up with the daily system activity.

I would estimate that to fully correct the current problems at hand, my staff would need at least two weeks time dedicated solely to these problems. If ongoing operations run perfectly from now on, this task will be a monumental one at best. Any further problems may put us in a position that may become extremely difficult if not impossible to fully recover from.

I cannot stress enough that the condition of the critical reporting function of the system remains unreliable and inaccurate in many respects. We can not give assurances as to the integrity of the system or it's reporting. It may be said that the "system" is in balance, but it becomes useless unless the "system" can produce reliable and accurate reports.

The problems noted above are all supported by documents in my Unit and are available for review if necessary.

EJM/ejm

cc: W. T. Drakeley
    A. S. Acayan
    J. B. Lewis ✓
    L. R. Scott

INTERDEPARTMENTAL MESSAGE
STO-201 REV. 7/86
(Stock No. 6938-051-01)

STATE OF CONNECTICUT

Obtain "STATE EMPLOYEE SUGGESTION" forms from, and send your ideas to: Employee's Suggestion Awards Program, 165 Capitol Avenue Hartford, Ct, 06106.

	NAME, TITLE	DATE
To	Unit Chiefs	May 18, 1988
	AGENCY, ADDRESS	
	Division of Special Revenue	
	NAME, TITLE	TELEPHONE
From	Orlando P. Ragazzi, Executive Director *Orlando P. Ragazzi*	566-2757
	AGENCY, ADDRESS	
	Division of Special Revenue	

Subject: Media Inquiries - Agency Coordination of Information Gathering and Response Procedures

This is to advise you and your staff that all media inquiries, questions or requests for information concerning the various activities of your Units shall be directed to our Division public information officer, Edward Harrigan, for response. Mr. Harrigan's responsibility is to insure that all relevant information resident in the Division concerning a media inquiry, question or request for information is identified. Mr. Harrigan, in his role as Agency public information officer, will act as Division spokesperson in respect of all matters, questions or inquiries directed to this Agency of whatsoever nature or kind effective as of this date.

Thank you for your cooperation and consideration.

OPR:sja

cc: William T. Drakeley
Edward J. Harrigan
Paul D. Bernstein

INTERDEPARTMENTAL MESSAGE
STO-201 REV. 7/86
(Stock No. 6938-051-01)

STATE OF CONNECTICUT

Obtain "STATE EMPLOYEE SUGGESTION" forms from, and send your ideas to: Employee's Suggestion Awards Program, 165 Capitol Avenue Hartford, Ct, 06106.

To	NAME, TITLE Orlando P. Ragazzi, Executive Director	DATE May 23, 1988
	AGENCY, ADDRESS Division of Special Revenue	
From	NAME, TITLE J. Blaine Lewis, Jr., Lottery Chief	TELEPHONE 2912
	AGENCY, ADDRESS Division of Special Revenue	

Subject: Your Directive of May 18 - Media Contacts

I am writing to ask you to reconsider subject directive for the following reasons:

1. It is virtually impossible to operate a Lottery properly without direct contact with the media. It is essential that the media and the public have the utmost confidence in the Lottery. This objective cannot be achieved by hygienic, homogenized, handouts from a P.I.O. If this directive continues to be applied to me, I will the the only Lottery director in the United States and Canada who is forbidden to have contact with the media.

2. As you know, I receive many requests for public speaking engagements. Since I assume that subject directive by implication prohibits such activity, I must emphasize that this further erodes public confidence in the Lottery. The perception of the public and the media will be that I am hiding behind a P.I.O.

3. As President of the North American Association of State and Provincial Lotteries, I am the official spokesman for all lotteries in the United States and Canada. If this directive continues to be applied to me, I will be in the incongruous position of being able to speak for all lotteries in the United States and Canada except my own.

JBL:r

cc: William Drakeley
    Gregory Ziemak

INTERDEPARTMENTAL MESSAGE
STO 201 REV. 7/86
(Stock No. 6938-051-01)

STATE OF CONNECTICUT

Obtain "STATE EMPLOYEE SUGGESTION" forms from, and send your ideas to: Employee's Suggestion Awards Program, 165 Capitol Avenue Hartford, Ct, 06106.

	NAME, TITLE	DATE
To	Orlando P. Ragazzi, Executive Director	October 11, 1988
	AGENCY, ADDRESS Division of Special Revenue	
From	NAME, TITLE J. Blaine Lewis, Jr., Lottery Chief	TELEPHONE 2912
	AGENCY, ADDRESS Division of Special Revenue	

Subject:

I am writing in response to your memo of September 19, 1988 in which you reminded me that Lotto and Instant sales are down compared with last year. You did not mention Daily Numbers and Play 4 sales but it should be noted that combined Daily Numbers and Play 4 sales are also down if we take into account the fact that we have approximately 8% more sales terminals than we did last year.

An undated and unsigned monograph entitled "Lotto Lottery Sales Trends" which was presented by this agency to the Legislature's Public Safety Committee on September 15, 1988 was apparently intended to give the impression that the decline in lottery sales is nothing new and in the hope that the reader would infer that the on-line system problems had little or no effect. To this end the document is generously sprinkled with the term "declining growth rate". Lets be clear about this, "declining growth rate" does not mean that sales have been declining it means that sales have been increasing but at a lesser rate of increase than previously. It is true that before the installation of the new on-line system we had a declining growth rate. (After enjoying a 35% annual growth rate, it is very difficult to avoid a declining growth rate.) However, since the installation of the new system, we have had declining sales - there is a difference.

At this point it might be helpful to look at the sales history of the lottery (see attached graph). From 1980 to 1988 sales nearly quadrupled. The Connecticut Lottery was considered to be one of the top lotteries in the United States, indeed it would not be an exaggeration to say that it was a world-class lottery. In spite of our recent catastrophe, Fiscal year 87-88 was our eleventh consecutive record-breaking year for sales and transfers to the General Fund. FY87-88 would have been even better but for the problems which began on May 8 and reduced sales for the last eight weeks of the year. An objective observer would surely conclude that we have done very well for the past eight years and were in fact doing very well until May 8, 1988.

Beginning on May 8, 1988 the performance of our new on-line system has had a negative effect not only on on-line ticket sales but also on instant ticket sales. (Approximately 80% of instant tickets are sold by on-line agents.) Apologists for the new on-line system have said that when the problems are corrected the new system will be as good as the old system. This is not very reassuring since the new system is required by contract to be far superior to the old system. Without expending excessive energy beating a dead horse, the following incontrovertible facts should suffice to put the performance of the new on-line system in proper perspective:

-2-

Total Fiscal Year Sales

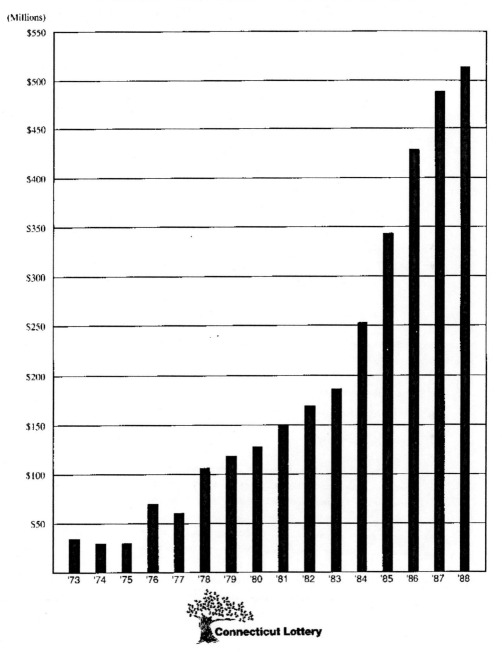

(Millions)

Connecticut Lottery

1. The penalties, when calculated will be very high.

2. The on-line vendor is recalling all of the sales terminals for extensive modifications.

During the past eight years, while the Lottery was compiling its enviable record, we in the lottery spent considerable time and energy to create good media relations and good public relations. This included many evening hours (including interrupted dinners) speaking with the media and many hours speaking to various groups ranging from service clubs to communion breakfasts. These efforts resulted, I believe, in a very good image for the Lottery. I believe that the media and the public trusted us. On May 18 you prohibited us from speaking to the media and the public. I believe that as a result our image has suffered. It is perceived that we have something to hide. In our business, we must be like Caesar's wife.

To summarize, I believe that there are two reasons for the decline in lottery sales:

1. The lottery has an unsatisfactory on-line system.

2. The lottery has a poor image.

- 3 -

To restore the lottery to its former position, I recommend the following:

1. Replace the on-line vendor as quickly as is practical.

2. Permit lottery personnel to speak for the lottery and to make public appearances.

3. Eliminate the plethora of committees and consultants and return the management of the lottery to the people who have operated it successfully for the past eight years.

4. Lend your support to enabling legislation to permit us to join a multi-state organization when conditions are right.

5. Put the full force of your office behind my efforts to refill a critical marketing position.

We are, as you know, planning changes in our instant game strategy in an attempt to increase instant game sales. We hope that this will, to some degree, ameliorate our problem but should not be considered to be a solution to the basic problems listed above.

cc: W. T. Drakeley
    G. P. Ziemak
    Al Acayan
    Ed Harrigan

170

INTERDEPARTMENTAL MESSAGE
STO-201 REV. 7/84
(Stock No. 6930-051-01)

STATE OF CONNECTICUT

Obtain "STATE EMPLOYEE SUGGESTION" forms from, and send your ideas to: Employee's Suggestion Awards Program, 165 Capitol Avenue Hartford, Ct, 06106.

	NAME, TITLE	DATE
To	Unit Chiefs	January 4, 198
	AGENCY, ADDRESS	
	Division of Special Revenue	
	NAME, TITLE	TELEPHONE
From	Orlando P. Ragazzi, Executive Director	
	AGENCY, ADDRESS	
	Division of Special Revenue	

Subject: Media Inquiries - Agency Coordination of Information Gathering and Response Procedures

This is to advise you and your staff that all media inquiries, questions or requests for information concerning the various activities of your Units shall be directed to our Division public information officer, Edward Harrigan, for response. Mr. Harrigan's responsibility is to insure that all relevant information resident in the Division concerning a media inquiry, question or request for information is identified. Mr. Harrigan, in his role as Agency public information officer, will act as Division spokesperson in respect of all matters, questions or inquiries directed to this Agency of whatsoever nature or kind effective as of this date.

The designation of a Public Information Officer as spokesman for the Division of Special Revenue does not in any way abridge an individual employee's right of freedom of speech, as guaranteed in Article 1 of the Amendments to the Constitution of the United States and in Sections 4 and 5 of the Declaration of Rights in the Constitution of the State of Connecticut. Each employee is at liberty to exercise his or her right of free speech in responding to inquiries about the Division's operations or expressing the employee's opinions about Division programs, projects, policies or decisions.

In doing so, the employee will be speaking as an individual, not as a representative of the Division, unless that employee is designated to announce or explain Division programs, projects, policies or decisions. When speaking as an individual, the employee may identify the position he or she holds in the Division. The employee must state clearly however, that in expressing opinions or making statements the employee is not acting as a spokesman for the Division or purporting to express its views or policies. If however, you are directed or authorized by appropriate Division officials to discuss issues with the media that involve your area of expertise, please exercise all the rules of good communication. When speaking on behalf of the Division, state only known _facts_, use good judgment and appropriate discretion, and be succinct and courteous.

Thank you for your cooperation and consideration.

Orlando P. Ragazzi
Executive Director

INTERDEPARTMENTAL MESSAGE
STO-201 REV. 7/86
(Stock No 6938-051-01)

STATE OF CONNECTICUT

Obtain "STATE EMPLOYEE SUGGESTION" forms from, and send your ideas to: Employee's Suggestion Awards Program, 165 Capitol Avenue Hartford, Ct, 06106.

To	NAME, TITLE Orlando P. Ragazzi, Executive Director	DATE February 7, 1989
	AGENCY, ADDRESS Division of Special Revenue	

From	NAME, TITLE J. Blaine Lewis, Jr., Lottery Chief	TELEPHONE 2912
	AGENCY, ADDRESS Division of Special Revenue	

Subject:

Your memo of January 24, 1989

Subject memo inquires about the history of our lotto game changes. Before responding I would like to offer the following comments:

In the spring of 1988, the Connecticut Lottery was completing its eleventh consecutive record-breaking year and its first half billion dollar year. It was number two in the United States in per capita revenue production and its lotto game was number one in the United States in per capita sales. In addition the lottery chief was in possession of a certificate issued by the State of Connecticut for "excellent managerial performance".

On May 8, 1988 the lottery's new on-line lottery system became operational and almost immediately serious system problems surfaced. Bizarre events followed. It was discovered that the lottery, which had appeared to be doing very well, had actually been suffering from a "declining growth rate" (a diabolically deceptive term). It was also discovered that the lottery chief who had been recently certified as an excellent manager was in fact not giving the lottery the management attention that it deserved. The state police then became involved and discovered that the technical competence and attitude of the lottery chief deserved their criticism. And now the latest, and hopefully the last, in this series of bizarre events is the effort to demonstrate a need to change the design of the lotto game even though it is the best lotto game in the country in spite of the on-line system problems.

It appears that this series of events which could be called "Operation Smokescreen" serves only to attempt to hide the bad decision involved in the awarding of the on-line contract.

Even though you did not inquire about the genesis of our lotto game, I believe that a review of our start up would be helpful.

When we started lotto in November of 1983, there were very few games in the country. They existed in states which were much larger in population than Connecticut and unfortunately they all had very low per capita sales.

Lotto is a population-based game. It is much easier to design a lotto game for California with a population of 27 million than for Delaware with a population of 660 thousand. The reality in designing a lotto game is that in order to achieve high ticket sales a large prize is required and in order to have a large prize, it is necessary to achieve high ticket sales. The smaller the population -- the more difficult the problem.

With a population as small as ours, it was not at all certain that a successful game could be created. In spite of this, we decided that our objective would be to "play big league lotto in a small state". We defined big league lotto as a game with routine million dollar prizes and occasional multi-million dollar prizes.

The three legs on the lotto stool are: population, probability of winning, and the luck of the draw. We intuitively knew, that if these three factors resulted in small prizes for an extended period of time, our objective would not be met. It was essential that the game design maximize the probability of prizes of at least one million dollars. Our intuition also told us that in a state as small as Connecticut traditional lotto game design would very likely result in a game with prizes too small to achieve our objective. Innovation was required. Our very small but very experienced lottery staff produced the required innovation. We devised a simple but effective plan which made it much more likely to have million dollar prizes. Our plan needed a name and our advertising agency suggested that we call it "the booster plan". The booster plan made it possible to achieve our objective. Simply put, it added dollars to the first prize pool, with certain limitations, when necessary to increase the first prize to one million dollars. Even though the added dollars were taken from the state's share, it was an excellent investment. The game started on November 7, 1983 and by December 23, just in time for Christmas, we had our first millionaire. The prize was in excess of $1.4 Million. We were off to a good start with weekly sales in the range of $500-600 thousand.

Approximately one year later, sales had increased to an average of over $2 Million per week. Sales had more than tripled since start up and they were still increasing. It appeared that we were about to outgrow the game. Now was the time to consider decreasing the probability of winning. We had the momentum and with weekly sales over $2 million, the danger of getting into trouble by overuse of the booster plan was minimal. We decided to "bite the bullet" and decrease the probability of winning. The next decisions to be made were: how much? and how should it be accomplished? It was fairly easy to answer the second question. It seemed obvious that increasing the quantity of numbers to be selected by the player was not the way to go since this would tend to emphasize the lower probability of winning. The new game then would be 6 of something. We wanted to lower the probability enough to keep the game growing but not enough to discourage the players. After much deliberation we narrowed our choices to a field of either 39 or 40. A game of 6/39 would result in a probability of 1/3.3 million and a game of 6/40 would result in a probability of 1/3.8 million. We were greatly concerned about being overly aggressive since that is a very easy way to kill a lotto game.

After still more deliberation and consideration of the effect of quick pick, we decided to go with 6/40. As we moved into calendar 1985 sales continued to increase, drawings with no rollovers were producing sales in excess of $2 Million so there was little likelihood of getting into trouble with the booster plan. The exact date (first drawing on April 12, 1985) was chosen to accommodate the preparations which were necessary and to put the launch of the new game beyond the Easter season.

The new game was well received and sales continued to increase. About that time some other states were launching twice-weekly lotto games and considerable pressure was put on the lottery unit to do the same. We successfully resisted this pressure. We felt that it was not safe to make the move at that time because of the danger of overuse of the booster plan. It was our position that we should not go to twice-a-week drawings until sales were over $3 Million per week. By the end of calendar 1985 sales had exceeded this level. Drawings with no rollover were producing sales of $3 Million. The exact date (first Tuesday drawing on April 8, 1986) was chosen to accommodate the preparations which were necessary and to put the launch of the new game beyond the Easter season.

The new game was very well received and sales continued to increase. The January 1987 issue of Gaming and Wagering Business reported that the Connecticut Lotto game was number one in the world in per capita sales. Even now, in spite of our trauma, our lotto game is still number one in the United States in per capita sales and is 32% above average.

The foregoing is essentially all that I can provide in response to your request. The lottery has always lacked management depth. As you know, of the total of 31 managers and professionals in the Division of Special Revenue at the present time, the lottery unit has only 4. We do not have committees, teams and task forces to create paper mountains. We cannot locate any paperwork pertaining to our deliberations. I assume that there were "lap notes" but they apparently do not now exist.

In view of the fact that game design decisions have in the past been made by the lottery unit, and in view of the fact that they have been good decisions (sometimes made while successfully resisting pressure), I respectfully request that lottery game design decisions be left to the lottery professionals in the lottery unit.

cc: W. T. Drakeley
     G. P. Ziemak

INTERDEPARTMENTAL MESSAGE
STO-201 REV. 7/86
(Stock No. 6938-031-01)

STATE OF CONNECTICUT

Obtain "STATE EMPLOYEE SUGGESTION" forms from, and send your ideas to: Employee's Suggestion Awards Program, 165 Capitol Avenue Hartford, Ct, 06106.

	NAME, TITLE	DATE
To	Mr. J. Blaine Lewis, Jr., Unit Chief/Lottery	May 16, 1989
	AGENCY, ADDRESS	
	Division of Special Revenue	
	NAME, TITLE	TELEPHONE
From	William V. Hickey, Executive Director	
	AGENCY, ADDRESS	
	Division of Special Revenue	

Subject: Lotto

The Division of Special Revenue is changing the "Lotto" game from a board size of six of forty to six of forty-four. The change will be submitted to the Gaming Policy Board for ultimate approval.

October 1, 1989 will be the date for implementation of the new "Lottery" game, subsequent to Gaming Policy Board approval. I am ordering you to assume the role of Project Manager for this transition and am directing you to draft an action plan which will delineate each step in the change process. The plan should minimally include the shortest timeframe in which this change can be effected, if in fact the General Instrument contract must be changed and if so how, the best method of marketing the change, and any additional equipment which must be procured. I will expect this draft to be submitted to me by May 31, 1989. If you are unable to meet this deadline, please advise me as soon as possible.

Feel free to select a Project Team and submit their names to me by May 26, 1989. I will inform their Unit Chief of the appointment and insure that they are made available to you.

I expect all your efforts will be expended towards a successful Lotto game transition.

William V. Hickey

WVH:sja

INTERDEPARTMENTAL MESSAGE
STO-201 REV 7/86
(Stock No. 6938 051 07)

STATE OF CONNECTICUT

Obtain "STATE EMPLOYEE SUGGESTION" forms from, and send your ideas to: Employee's Suggestion Awards Program, 165 Capitol Avenue Hartford, Ct. 06106.

To	**NAME, TITLE** William V. Hickey, Executive Director	**DATE** May 17, 1989
	AGENCY, ADDRESS Division of Special Revenue	
From	**NAME, TITLE** J. Blaine Lewis, Jr.	**TELEPHONE** 2912
	AGENCY ADDRESS Division of Special Revenue	

Subject:

I am writing in response to your memo of May 16, 1989 in which you ordered a change in our Lotto game. I would prefer to have a bit more time to respond to such a critical decision but because you have issued an oral order to respond today by 4:00 P.M., I am rushing my response in order to comply.

I do not, on principle, oppose changes in our Lotto game. Our present very successful game is our third version of Lotto. As you know, I have offered to design a new Lotto game to put on the shelf to be used when we outgrow our present game. However, I do oppose any change in the game at this time.

Since Lotto is the Lottery's biggest money maker and since the Lottery contributes approximately 84% of the revenue produced by the Division of Special Revenue, any change in this game should be very carefully considered and must, of course, be approved by the Gaming Policy Board.

I am especially troubled by the minimal role of the Board in this proposed game change. There are only two Board members remaining and one has announced his intention to leave. If we proceed with preparations to change this game, we will be creating a very awkward situation. We will be asking the Board to consent to a game change about which four of the five members were not able to advise. Because this proposed change is so critical and controversial, I believe that the citizens of the state would be better served if the entire new Board was permitted to advise and consent on this matter _after_ hearing all of the facts. I believe that this is especially important since this proposed change is being thrust upon the Lottery. This is a departure from the usual procedure. In the past all of the Lottery Game Designs, which have made our Lotto game number one in the world in per capita sales and have made our Lottery number two in the United States in per capita revenue production, originated in the Lottery.

In view of the foregoing, I respectfully request that you withdraw your order of May 16, 1989.

cc: W. T. Drakeley
     G. P. Ziemak
     A. J. Mazzola

APPENDIX

INTERDEPARTMENTAL MESSAGE
STO-201 REV. 7/86
(Stock No. 6938-051-01)

STATE OF CONNECTICUT

Obtain "STATE EMPLOYEE SUGGESTION" forms from, and send your ideas to: Employee's Suggestion Awards Program, 165 Capitol Avenue Hartford, Ct, 06106.

	NAME, TITLE	DATE
To	Mr. J. Blaine Lewis, Jr., Unit Head/Lottery	May 22, 1989
	AGENCY, ADDRESS Division of Special Revenue, 555 Russell Road, Newington, CT 06111	

	NAME, TITLE	TELEPHONE
From	William V. Hickey, Executive Director	
	AGENCY, ADDRESS *William V. Hickey 5.22.89* Division of Special Revenue, 555 Russell Road, Newington, CT 06111	

Subject:

Pursuant to Division of Special Revenue Personnel Procedure No. 1., you are notified that a pre-disciplinary hearing has been scheduled for Wednesday, May 24, 1989 at 1:00 p.m. in my office at Division Headquarters in Newington. Whether or not you wish to appear at this hearing is your choice. Connecticut General Statutes §5-202(j), entitles you to representation of your own choosing.

At this hearing, the following charges against you will be discussed:

On May 18, 1989 you refused to comply with a lawful, direct order.

This hearing will verify the facts and provide you with the opportunity to relate your side of the story and comment on the disciplinary action that may be imposed. Disciplinary action in the form of termination from state service is being considered. After this hearing (assuming you want this hearing held), a decision will be made about the specific disciplinary action to be taken, if any. You are encouraged to attend this hearing.

I acknowledge receipt of this memorandum.

Signature _____ Date __5/22/89__

WVH:sja

cc: Official Personnel File

I request additional time to prepare and obtain counsel
BL.

177

SUMMARY OF SALES
AND NET REVENUES TO STATE
FISCAL YEARS 1988 - 95[1]

Fiscal Year July 1-June 30	Gross Sales	Net Revenue to State
1987-88 (Base year)	$259,347,000	$115,100,000
1988-89	$236,011,000	$105,400,000
1989-90	$232,860,000	$ 98,700,000
1990-91	$219,506,000	$ 95,200,000
1991-92	$219,794,000	$ 93,150,000
1992-93	$202,474,000	$ 84,200,000
1993-94	$153,699,000	$ 64,750,000
1994-95	$170,456,205	$ 70,850,000

Fiscal Year	Annual Difference in Sales	Annual Difference in Net Revenue
1988-89	-$ 23,336,000	-$ 9,700,000
1989-90	-$ 26,487,000	-$16,400,000
1990-91	-$ 39,841,000	-$19,900,000
1991-92	-$ 39,553,000	-$21,950,000
1992-93	-$ 58,873,000	-$30,900,000
1993-94	-$105,648,000	-$50,350,000
1994-95	-$ 88,890,795	-$44,250,000
TOTAL AMOUNT OF ANNUAL DIFFERENCE FROM 1987-88	**-$382,628,795**	**-$193,450,000**

---

[1] In January, 1988, the LOTTO contractor was changed from GTech to General Instruments; In May, 1988, General Instrument was allowed to activate its systems and take over LOTTO operations resulting in a system wide breakdown that was not fully corrected until February, 1989; and in May, 1989, the LOTTO game format was changed; all over the objections of the plaintiff, J. Blaine Lewis, Jr., who until May, 1989, when he was terminated by the defendants Cowen, Lange and Hickey, was Chief of the Lottery Unit. Sales and net revenues had risen in every year through the 1987-88 fiscal year, See Bar Chart, Exhibit M, In Opposition to Summary Judgment. Lotto revenues have gone down substantially in every year since these changes were recommended by the Executive Director and approved by Messrs. Cowen, Lange and Hickey, as members of the Gaming Policy Board and Executive Director, respectively.

"THE SET"

WEEKLY LOTTERY

MAY 6, 1981

DRAKELEY

350,000
PLUS

LEWIS

275,000
OR LESS

WITNESSES

John Conkling
George Cooper
Robert James
James O'Connell
David Sheehan

ATTEST:

A. W. OPPENHEIMER

Printed in the United States
2268

9 781930 859128